Top-Gun Selling

Tactics of the
Top 2% of Salespeople

Top Gun Selling

Tactics of the
Top 2% of Salespeople

William H. Blades

iv

International Standard Book Number: 1-878182-15-3

Printed in the United States of America

Dedication

This book is dedicated to the sales professionals who give their very best talents to their clients day in and day out. You are the ones that bring credit to our wonderful profession. I take my hat off to you!

Acknowledgement

I thank my parents for bringing me into this wonderful world. Special thanks to those that help me with my skills and gave me the opportunity to grow. Early in my career, Elmer Mantey gave me the chance to head up a sales and marketing group. We gave each other our best and I am grateful for his tutoring. Somers White encouraged me to begin speaking and consulting. I have learned much from him about serving others and driving hard to reach one's goals.

Saving the best for last, I thank God for the talent he gave me to serve others.

Table Of Contents

Get Committed To Getting Organized • Develop An Annual
Sales Plan • Set Specific Goals • Get A System – Paper Or
Electronic • Gather All Tools • Schedule Your Time
Carefully • Schedule Time For Professional Growth • Make
Choices About People • Review Your Plan And
Organization Frequently

Keep Graphs To Measure Productivity • Use Codes To Help
You Prioritize • Time Management • Make The Most Of
Fridays • Personal Time • Combine Business And Pleasure •
Plan And Manage Your Time On Paper

Learn About The Organization • Find The Decision-Makers •
Get To Know The Troops • Bring A Benefit • Confirm The
Appointment • Send Background Information In Advance •
List Objectives For Each Call • Plan Your Travel • That First
Impression • Preparation Action Steps

Finding Prospects • Newspapers And Trade Magazines •
Trade Associations And Civic Organizations • Trade Shows
• Yellow Pages • Get Referrals From Clients • Contact
Associations In Allied Industries • Divide And Conquer •
Timing Is Everything • Abandon Fear • Energize Your Effort
• Follow Up Fast

Be Open To Change • Practice Brings Improvement • Do
Whatever It Takes • Handling Rejection • Never Discount
Luck • Bad Attitudes Are Bad For Business And Your
Health • The Can Do Attitude • Bounce Back, Bounce Up •
Find A Coach, Not A Couch • Work On Your Attitude •
Take An Attitude Check

CHAPTER ONE

Get Organized

Your selling effort will never be victorious without a good battle plan and the discipline to follow through. If you want to improve your personal selling skills, it is unlikely you can advance beyond your current levels of accomplishment without getting organized. Extremely organized! When you are organized, you'll be more productive. What's more, your efforts will succeed because you'll be able to take care of the details that often mean the difference between closing the sale or losing the deal.

Almost all successful people have role models and mentors. One of my role models told the following story.

> *Many years ago, a baseball game was in the bottom of the ninth inning and the score was tied. There were three balls and two strikes on the batter. With the next pitch, the batter hit a deep fly ball to right center field and after rounding first, second, and then third base, the batter slid into home base in a cloud of dust well before the ball arrived. The umpire shouted as loud as he could, "he's out!" The fans went crazy because the*

batter looked as if he was clearly safe. The fans began to boo and throw paper cups and other litter on the field in the umpire's direction. The umpire explained, "The batter is out because he failed to touch first base."

This story is a metaphor for the process of selling. The message is simple. You must pay attention to every little step in the selling process to score big when it counts. Missing any of the small details along the way might cost dearly in the end. Getting organized and staying focused is critical if you want to stay on top of the details necessary for effective selling. Getting organized will help you earn additional income and take much of the stress out of the effort to advance your career or grow your business.

Selling is much more fun for those who love what they do, have clear cut goals and are prepared to do all the little things that lead to eventual success. Three primary characteristics often separate the great performers in sales and management from the average ones. These characteristics are good communication skills, a team approach to getting things done, and the discipline to stay organized. You might be terrific at the first two things, but if you are not organized in your daily activities you will never meet your full potential for success. Getting organized starts with getting committed.

Get Committed To Getting Organized

Good organizational skills do not come easy for most people. Nevertheless, the incentive for developing better organizational skills are great, since they usually lead to more sales, higher income, less stress, and more time available for family and friends.

No matter how bright or talented individuals may be, most people's performance will be mediocre without impeccable organization. Experts claim in the course of an average career, most business professionals will waste as much as one year's time searching through clutter on their desks! With some attention to organization, that time could be spent prospecting for new customers or closing sales with current ones. If you are not as organized as you should be, it's time to get committed! The first step is to develop a plan.

Develop An Annual Sales Plan

All successful selling efforts start with a simple action plan; one laid out for an entire year. By developing a one-year sales plan, you can work the plan backwards and list all the major things you wish to accomplish by the quarter, the month and the week. As each quarter or month approaches you will not lose sight of where your plan is taking you. By planning for the year, you're able to ask yourself this question every week – 'What is it I'm going to do next week that will make a big difference at the end of the year and help me reach the goals I've set for myself?"

Take time to develop your plan. Your plan should include your general business and sales goals. It also must include tactics you will employ and specific action steps you will take to execute the plan.

Schedule thinking time regularly: to review your plan and make necessary adjustments. Almost all of this planning and thinking time should be done at night or on Saturdays – never between the hours of 8:00 AM to 5:00 PM, Monday through Friday. That's customer time!

I lived for a time in Memphis, Tennessee. A homeowner in the community added a new wing to his house annually. The house was constantly undergoing an expansion, and these expansions drove the neighbors crazy. Additions to the house were in a wide variety of shapes, including rectangles, squares, circles, and even triangles. The design was chaotic and the house bordered on being an eye sore. Personally, I felt the homeowner could benefit from professional psychological help aimed at balancing both the creative and logical sides of his brain. Even so, the point of the story is simple. If you do not have a written plan to increase sales and revenue, you will drift about building a business or a career that doesn't turn out exactly like you hoped.

Set Specific Goals

Goals are planned for events that should motivate you to become the person it takes to reach them. Whether they are company goals for overall performance or personal sales goals, they must be realistic and attainable, yet expansive enough to stretch your abilities. Therefore, when you work on achieving your goals, you need not ask yourself, "What do I want to achieve?" You know, because it is in your plan. Be specific when you develop goals for your plan.

Early in my career, I attended a seminar presented by The Franklin Institute on the subject of time management. The instructor gave a very vivid example underscoring the value of goals. He stated that when a goal is valued, it becomes a priority. To illustrate his point, he told the following audience participation story. He asked everyone in the audience who had a young child to raise a hand. He selected one individual and asked for the child's name. Then, he told this story.

> *"Sir," he said, "you and I will go to Chicago and we will get on top of two skyscrapers. You will be on top of one building and I will be on top of the one next to it. A steel I-beam connects the top of both buildings."*

> *He then asked the gentleman if he would be willing to cross from one building to the other walking on the I-beam, which was only six inches wide, for a reward of $100. The man, of course, replied that he would not. The offer was then increased to $10,000. However, to earn the money he would have to cross the I-beam while it was snowing and sleeting and the wind would be blowing approximately 50 miles per hour. He still refused.*

*Then, he told the man he would take his young child to
the top of his building and would drop the child to the
street if the man would not cross that I-beam to get his
child. He asked the audience member again, "Now,
would you come across?" The man replied, "In a heart
beat."*

The instructor clearly illustrated the value this man had for
his child. The child's security and happiness was a powerful
goal, which would motivate him to act in an extraordinary way.
Never underestimate the importance goals, values, and priorities
have in shaping motivations and actions. Once you develop a
plan with several goals, examine the values behind them and set
priorities accordingly.

When I am conducting a sales training session, I tell the
same story from time to time. Once I asked for someone in the
audience to tell me if he would cross the I-beam to save his child.
He hollered out, "which one of my kids do you have?" I loved
it.

Your plan can include many specific goals, such as what
time you are going to get up, how many contacts you are going
to make daily or how many new client visits you will make
monthly, quarterly and annually. Another goal that should be in
your plan is the number of prospect calls you will make
annually. Setting specific goals for customer or prospect contacts
makes it easy to set targets by quarters, months and weeks. That
way, you can monitor the number of calls you make and keep on
track with your goals.

Smart sales people understand that prospecting is the
lifeblood of their profession. Great sales efforts start with a plan
that emphasizes specific goals for prospecting. Also, set goals
for the number of new customers and the sales volume you wish
to achieve for the year. Write all priority goals on paper and
place your written goals where you can see them daily.

Write your goals on a 3" x 5" card and place the card with a rubber band on the sun visor of your car. Put your goals in your PC or notebook computer. Handwrite them on a page of your day planner. Post them on or above your desk where you will see them everyday. Carry a copy in your briefcase, so you'll have a reminder at home or when traveling. Soon your goals will become programmed, not only into your conscious mind, but into your subconscious mind as well. If you're serious about your goals, keeping them in sight will help you stay focused and on track. Distractions will not be a powerful issue when your goals are clear and constantly visible.

Set a realistic goal for the number of new clients you will bring on board for the year and the dollar volume in sales each will provide. For example, you might state in your plan, "I will bring on 40 new clients during the next business year, each placing minimum orders of $25,000." Specific goals will force you to pinpoint your efforts, helping you to select the specific prospects with whom to invest your time and talents. To reach the goal in the above example, for instance, it will be necessary to land 10 new customers each quarter or three to four new customers each month.

I recommend your plan be simple, realistic and focused on the most important goals and objectives. Some successful sales people, however, develop very detailed plans. They include in their plans how much income they're planning on and how many hours they will work each day. Whatever your goals, be sure to have them in writing, so they're constantly in front of you. When you are on the road and you have faced some rejection, reviewing your goals and your overall performance to date can be comforting. If you're making progress toward reaching your goals, a few setbacks won't become completely demoralizing for you or your troops.

Once I asked a sales person, "What are your goals?" He replied, "To grow up and be the kind of person my dog thinks

I am." I remember laughing when he said that. I also knew this person well enough to understand this probably was his only goal. Goals can be the motivator for success. They can force you to develop a battle plan for reaching them and help you stay focused along the way. If your goals are limited, so will be your accomplishments.

Again, reduce your plan to its essence and fit your primary goals on a 3" x 5" card. Then, fasten the card next to your telephone. Although more symbolic than practical, by doing so you will never lose sight of your goals.

Remember, once your specific sales goals are set, reaching them will be determined by the value you bring to your clients and customers. That notion can be the philosophy by which you conduct business, a pledge to deliver more value to every potential client than you have ever delivered before.

Get A System • Paper Or Electronic

Now that you have a plan with clear goals and have made a commitment to get organized, the next step is to get a system. You can't stay on top of details without a system to help.

If your employer does not provide you with a standard account form, you should prepare your own. The form should include basic information about the prospect or customer. Such information might be the company name, bill to address, ship to address, contacts with correct titles and telephone numbers along with their personal interests and birthdays. Other information to include is the name of the vendor from whom they currently buy, what they buy and how much. Create a large section on this form to write all the things you want to learn once you have an opportunity to make contact with a company buyer or representative.

Each form should have a place to classify existing or prospective accounts. Once you have obtained some basic information, classify each account as A, B, or C. Accounts classified as "A" have the most potential to impact the bottom line and your take home pay. "B" accounts are the next priority, while "C" accounts should be worked using the least time consuming and least costly sales methods.

One section of the form can indicate the primary buying habits of the prospect. For example, you may want to list such words as "quality," "price," "convenience" or other factors that will be the primary influence in the purchasing decision. You can circle the one that best describes the account and later use the information to structure your sales presentation. You also might want to have a place on the form where you can describe the company by circling a word such as "progressive" or "stagnate." Another section could be an area where you circle the words "sell now" or "sell next year." If you like this idea, be sure to use codes on the forms because you would not want a customer to see your records and discover he was listed as a price buyer, or that the buyer's company was viewed as being stagnate. By having a system to document basic information, you can decide the amount of effort and resources you will commit to any particular prospect or client.

An increasing number of my clients are equipping their sales personnel with notebook computers or similar tools to capture crucial information and speed up the communication process. Computers are great. As their cost keeps tumbling, they make yesterday's mode of handling the sales process almost extinct. Computers speed up the process. When you feed in accurate data, they help to avoid miscommunication. In other words, invest in the latest technology to keep yourself on the cutting edge and help you effectively organize your effort.

A note of caution: a number of sales personnel take their notebook computers with them on client visits. Some, however, start entering data while the client is speaking. If you are fast at entering data, doing so might be okay. However, if you must slow the verbal exchange in order to trap everything in the computer, you are being unprofessional and rude. Don't make the client slow down for your benefit. Take notes and input the data in your notebook computer immediately following the meeting.

My personal preference is, whenever possible, to utilize a computer before 8 AM and after 5 PM. To me, time with clients is time to utilize your brain, ears and belly – not a gizmo. If you are not ready to enter the age of information technology; then, by all means, set up a paper system that will keep you on track and help you with necessary follow-up.

Gather All Your Tools

Half of getting organized is having all the selling ammunition you need at your fingertips at all times. Organize a place in your office to store and inventory your sales literature, price lists, samples, order forms, credit applications, promotional items and supplies such as note cards, post cards, business cards and stationery. If you use audio/visual aids in your sales presentation, they should be kept close at hand, too.

Nothing can cut into the effectiveness of the selling process as time wasted looking for sales tools only to discover you have run out. Having them organized in a place of immediate access will make it easy to keep track of your supply and order more long before the supply is exhausted. Never be in the position to lose a sale because you couldn't respond immediately to a request for product information. Your briefcase is your office away from home. Stock it carefully with your sales materials. Then, inventory and replenish your supply weekly.

Schedule Your Time Carefully

Since selling is a numbers game, setting goals for the number of contacts you will make daily or weekly, is a must. Good organization can help you achieve the maximum number of calls. If you are calling on customers and prospects in the field, map your territory carefully and schedule appointments to get the most personal sales calls from every trip out of the office. Quite simply, your objective is to achieve less driving time and more time with customers or prospects. When on maneuvers, get there fast and come with a full array of ammo.

Most sales representatives are better off leaving their territories at noon on a Friday and going to their desks to set up appointments for the next week, return phone calls, get out mail, and do other miscellaneous duties that are necessary components of the sales process. When you think about it, few new orders are ever closed on a Friday afternoon. That's because most buyers usually are busy trying to wrap up the week's efforts in order to get a fresh start on Monday.

Most sales people have reports that they must turn in to their employer. If this is your situation, build a track record for yourself by always doing reports correctly, legibly and on time. To save time for clients you may be able to fill out some of your reports during lunch. The objective is to always get your reports completed and delivered when requested. Not only are you getting things done on time, you'll be submitting your written reports when most facts are still clear in your mind. If you try to fill out a call report or account record two or three weeks after the call, the chances of remembering all of the important details of the contact will be slim. Friday afternoons and Saturday mornings are the best time to complete these tasks.

Administration of the sales effort also involves correspondence with customers and prospects such as letters, cards, mailgrams, faxes, newsletters, thank you notes and greeting cards. Again, Friday afternoons and Saturday mornings are great times to do these mailings. Each mailer represents an extra contact you have made with a client or prospect and also enables you to keep your name and product in the mind of the buyer.

Remember, hand-written notes have much more impact than a formal letter because the client knows you personally took time to write rather than have a secretary send a form letter. If your handwriting is atrocious and you would rather compose a note on your computer, be sure to include something of a personal nature so the reader will know it could only have come from you.

Schedule Time For Professional Growth

If you're organized, you also should be able to schedule time for personal growth. How many books have you read recently relating to sales and business management? How many audiocassette tapes on these topics have you listened to in the last quarter? Keep up with what's going on in your industry by subscribing to at least five or six trade magazines. Most trade magazines are free. I get more than 200 trade magazines sent to my office. They cover a wide range of businesses and industries. I get great ideas from the articles I read, and I also am able to keep track of trends in the industry, growth of corporations, promotions of key personnel and a whole host of other valuable information. You also should be reading everything you can about your profession, your industry and current business topics in the territory in which you work. Mark Twain once commented, "The man who doesn't read has no advantage over the man who cannot read."

Make Choices About People

Charlie Jones, a professional speaker and businessman, said, "You are today what you will be in five years, except for two things – the people you meet and the books you read." Therefore, you might ask yourself this question. "With whom am I hanging around and what are they doing for me?" You should "hang around" people who positively stretch your character and abilities and people who will tell you the truth rather than only what you would like to hear. Schedule time with quality people, there's so little time to waste with people who will never help you to be your best.

Review Your Plan And Organization Frequently

Set up a review system to compare your current results with the goals you set at the beginning of the year. I suggest a review of goals and corresponding progress on a monthly basis. Never wait for the ninth or tenth month of the year when it's too late to make appropriate changes. If you see you're falling significantly behind, take time to evaluate what's not working and be honest with yourself based on your performance. Know where you stand. Don't wait for the boss to tell you that you've done well and certainly don't wait for the boss to tell you that you're behind. If you're the boss, be honest about where you are spending your time and energy. By having your own reward and reprimand system in place, you will be exercising self-control.

When you're ahead of planned goals, be sure to celebrate the victories. Especially when things in the past have been difficult. For example, select ways to celebrate the landing of a new order. Buy yourself a gift or treat yourself and a guest to dinner at a nice restaurant. On the other hand, be sure to have a system in place to reprimand yourself when things are not going as well as planned. If you are a member of a sales staff, be sure to ask your boss or your mentor for frequent feedback. Most likely, if things are not progressing positively, it's probably because you are not as organized and efficient as you should be.

CHAPTER TWO

Time Management and Productivity

Time passes equally for all men and women. Each day is 24 hours long, no matter who you are or what may be your talents or position. Time can be either an ally or an enemy. To get the most from life, time should never be wasted. That doesn't mean every waking hour must be devoted to your business or your career. It means getting the most from each day, so you can balance your life and have time for family and personal interests.

Most sales people lose an average of two to three hours each day doing meaningless things and not doing the productive things that can help them succeed. If developing a plan and getting organized is the first step, managing time and increasing productivity is the next step to selling success.

Your goals may be very clear and your intentions stellar, but that's not enough. There's no free lunch and every successful person pays a price for success. To be successful, you must be willing to pay the price first and reward yourself afterward. Reach some short-term goals and then play golf or go shopping. Reach some larger goals and take a day off to go to the beach. You can reward yourself with a new outfit or a mini-vacation after you make significant progress. Never get into the habit of rewarding yourself on the come; that is, taking your reward before you close the sale or reach your sales goals. Many hopefuls have treated themselves right out of a job or a business.

Keep Graphs To Measure Productivity

Keep current graphs to record your sales effort. While computer print outs showing progress are terrific, simple graphs paint a very explicit picture. Every serious sales professional should keep a monthly line graph showing sales for last year, this year's projections and actual sales to date for the current year. By using a different color for each line on the graph, you can see with a quick glance how well you're progressing. Also, consider keeping a graph on the number of new customers you acquire each month or new prospects you have contacted.

To be productive in sales remember the following:

- Set long-range goals and review them regularly.
- Set specific objectives — short-term and long-term.
- Determine what resources are required to reach your goals.
- Anticipate as many obstacles as possible and make plans to overcome them.
- Prioritize, prioritize, prioritize.
- Manage your time, spending it on priority tasks first.

Productivity and success are possible only when you are willing to prioritize your activities and accomplish first those that will have the greatest impact on reaching your goals. Here are some ideas on productivity:

1. Study successful people. Study people who are successful to determine how they do it.
2. Understand the needs and motivations of your major customers and hottest prospects; doing so will make your selling effort more successful.

3. Don't spend major time on minor things. Spend less time on administration and more time with prospects and customers and with the process of selling.

4. Don't spend major dollars on minor things. Focus your resources where you can get the most from your investment.

5. Life gets better when you get better. Improving performance will bring the rewards worthy of the effort. To get better, however, requires dedication and practice.

6. Welcome change. Without a willingness to change the way you do things, the next five years will be the same as the last five. Work harder on changing yourself and be willing to try different approaches.

7. Seek new ideas, and implement those that can make a difference. It's often a few simple ideas that can help you achieve remarkable success. Do something with the new ideas that make sense for you, your company and your selling effort.

8. Planning improves the chances for positive results in the future. Along with determining your specific selling goals and objectives, develop an action plan, which lists everything you will do to reach them.

9. Do the ordinary things in an extraordinary way. Never fail to do the basic things that lead to the sale, but try to put your own original twist on them.

10. Never stop learning. Invest at least one hour each week in education and self-improvement.

11. Stick to your plan. Your plan will help you determine which activities to undertake.

12. Saturday is not a holiday. Saturday is the day to prepare for success. Use Saturday morning for planning, reviewing, and administration.

13. Study ants. Everybody, especially lazy people, can take inspiration from watching hard-working ants. You'll be successful only if you're willing to work hard and smart.

14. Five minutes spent complaining is five minutes wasted. When others want to waste time complaining, stop them with a phrase like, "What's the solution?"

Jim Rohn, a successful consultant, shares many of the above ideas with his clients. They worked for me, and they will work for you, too.

Use Codes To Help You Prioritize

To use time wisely, you must prioritize. Assign a code to all of your accounts and activities. A simple code might be the letters A, B or C. For example an "A" account would represent a very large client or prospect, "B" would be medium-sized accounts and "C" would be small accounts. When getting started, most sales people must spend a fair amount of time with B and C accounts. Smaller accounts often appreciate the extra efforts to serve them and sales people can develop and improve their skills and credibility dealing with smaller customers before moving on to the larger ones. Later as the business grows or a sales person is more successful at landing and serving "A" accounts, time and effort allocations can be shifted. Be sure not to let very small customers chew up the time that should be devoted to "A" accounts.

Time Management

When scheduling appointments, do not forget the "30-30-30" rule. I often encounter sales people who like to drop by the establishment of an existing client just to say, "hello." More often than not, I find they do this with smaller clients or clients with which they are friends. The "30-30-30" rule is simple. They will often take 30 minutes to stop by and see Jim, another 30 minutes waiting to see Jim and another 30 minutes to get back on track. That is 90 minutes wasted! If you are guilty of this, try to calculate how many times you have done this in the past month. The number of times probably will be astounding! Time is money; don't waste it with unproductive activity.

Here's an example to consider. I hired a sales representative to cover the city of Chicago and the states of Wisconsin and Minnesota. I asked the sales person to spend approximately 75 percent of his time, for the first year, in Wisconsin and Minnesota. I made this request because sales representatives, in the same territory, would spend the vast majority of their time calling on headquarter accounts in Chicago. These accounts, while large, often require more calls. Usually, they also require lots of time and significant resources spent getting products or services approved. In the end, most purchases involve a bid format to obtain the order. I suggested our sales representative call on often-neglected, medium-sized accounts in the rural areas of Wisconsin and Minnesota. I was betting that during the winter, these accounts would not be properly serviced by representatives from other companies. So, what happened?

The sales representative asked us to furnish him with a four-wheel drive vehicle. Great idea! We got him the vehicle he wanted and it paid off. He spent the winter months making sales calls in rural Wisconsin and Minnesota and writing lots of orders. What were most of his competitors doing? They were sitting in Chicago calling clients to say they couldn't get there because of the "bad weather." Develop a strategy. Then, do what others are too lazy or too unwilling to do. It will pay off with a significant increase in sales.

Make the Most of Fridays

Want to do a better job at managing time and boosting your overall effectiveness? Don't make sales calls on Friday afternoon. When you think about it, most clients are trying to wrap up the week and few major decisions are made on a Friday. Consequently, I believe Friday is a good day to catch up, maintain and to move things ahead.

If you stay at home or in the office on Friday, you can make 25 to 50 outbound telephone calls. You also can send 10 to 20 notes to customers and prospects to stay in touch, confirm appointments, or send personal greetings such as birthday cards.

Fridays also are great days to prepare proposals, write letters of introduction, fill out call reports and complete other administrative tasks that will take thinking time. I also use Fridays to telephone customers and prospects to say "thank you" for orders, interest or courtesies extended during a sales call. Fridays also are great days for thinking and for reviewing your plan and your progress. Dedicate one hour on Friday to take a look at a map of your territory and to review your entire client and prospect lists. Think about things you can do differently to either make a sale or keep a customer.

For example, in 1993 floodwaters covered a vast area of the Midwestern United States. Newspapers and magazines were filled with accounts of the floods. Every night viewers witnessed the destruction caused by the floodwaters on television. That gave me an idea. I sent bottled water to two potential clients in Des Moines, Iowa. They appreciated the gift and my understanding of their awful experience. You see, ironically the floods were responsible for a severe shortage of drinking water. As a result of my simple gesture, I got two new clients!

Taking time to review progress also enables you to evaluate the accounts you have been calling on without success. Adjust your plan and determine which clients you will stop calling on and which new ones you should add to your list of prospects. If your type of business requires repetitive calls to get or keep a customer, and if nothing has happened after you have extended a reasonable effort, call the customer to have one last conversation before dropping all of your efforts.

The conversation might go as follows:

> *Mr. or Ms. Client, I have to make a decision regarding how I should be spending my time. I have been calling on you for X months or X years without success. Can I ask you a question? "Would you encourage me to*

continue to call on you? If so, what do I need to do differently in order to bring you on board as a satisfied customer?"

By listening carefully to the response, you can determine immediately if you should drop the prospect, put him on the back burner for a while or step up efforts to turn him into a customer.

Personal Time

Be sure to schedule some personal time in your tune management planning. Set aside time for fun, relaxation and personal growth. In order to grow personally and professionally and to improve your skills, you must continue your education. Attend seminars, read books and listen to audiotapes. Spend at least 30 minutes a day reading to stay abreast of business, local and national news. Listen to audiotapes in your car and turn your auto into a university on wheels. Listening daily for 10 or 15 minutes to instructional tapes should give you at least one practical, new idea each week.

You also need to get completely away from business from time to time to be effective. The U.S. Defense Department has rest and recreation centers all over the world for military personnel. They know that battle fatigue and excessive pressure can destroy a soldier and maybe those around him. For effectiveness, be sure to schedule sufficient R & R time.

Combine Business And Pleasure

Sometimes you can combine business and pleasure. Golf and tennis are two great ways to get exercise and relax. They also can provide a setting for getting orders. When playing golf or tennis with a customer or prospect, never be the one to bring up business. You won't have to, because the client almost always does! I have landed large orders for my business and for my clients on the golf course.

The best foursome for accomplishing business during a golf

game consists of two prospects, one very satisfied customer and you. You and a potential client are in one cart. In the second cart is the existing client paired with a prospect. The potential customer in the second cart will surely ask your existing customer lots of questions about you and your performance. In the meantime, you can discuss business with the prospect with whom you are paired.

A recent study showed 92 percent of golf playing business people felt playing golf with another businessperson promoted business relationships. Over half said they had received business orders as a result of playing golf with customers and prospects. That's all I needed to hear to encourage me to play more golf with my customers and prospects.

Playing golf or tennis with a client also enables you to be more creative in your conversations. That's because exercise releases endorphins and adrenaline that stimulates the brain and gets the body juices flowing. Exercise stimulates the right side, or creative side, of your brain. The next time your customer hits his ball in the lake, you could respond with something more humorous than, "Wow! You really hit that ball! Did you see how high the water splashed?"

Plan and Manage Your Time On Paper

When I ask struggling sales people why they don't keep an accurate, daily time management system, often they tell me they don't have time. That's a lame excuse! Buy and use the most sophisticated, daily time management planner you can afford. I suggest that you use a day planner that is large enough to write numerous details on any given daily page. At the beginning of the year, list birthdays of your immediate family so you have a reminder to try to make every effort to be home during those dates. If you're married, it makes good sense to also log your anniversary. Log all of the conventions and major events you plan to attend during the year. Having all of those dates scheduled will enable you to control the days just before those events and those, which immediately follow.

For example, if you live in Memphis and you were going to a convention in Nashville, first log the convention dates, such as November 12 through 15, as "convention, Nashville." The day before the convention and the day after you could plan to call on accounts while driving to and from Nashville. Schedule the sales appointments well in advance to make the most productive use of the travel time to and from your destination.

My day planner goes with me everywhere, seven days a week, 24 hours a day. Whenever an idea presents itself I write it in my day planner. Also, if I am at a social function and someone asks to get together at a later date, an appointment can be scheduled on the spot without requiring wasted time trying to schedule the meeting later.

I realize that many people now use computers for time management. The only challenge I see with computers is you cannot take them with you everywhere. I can take my day planner into a nice restaurant and place it out of sight. When an idea hits me I can pick up my day planner and write it down, so I never lose a good thought. Also, if I see somebody in the restaurant that would like to know if I can call them or come see them, I can open my day planner and schedule an appointment.

Keeping a detailed day planner also enables you to review your efforts at the end of the month. You can take a look at where you spent time and whether it was time well spent or time wasted. Study your routine very hard. You might even ask an associate to study it for you, so you can identify areas where time was wasted. Often a sales person finds he invested too much travel time making sales calls to low priority prospects, when the telephone or the mail system could have handled them just as well and at much less cost of time and money.

Time is money! The following chart shows what must be

earned each hour to support an income. If you are making $40,000 a year and want to make $75,000 annually, you must value every hour you work as worth $38.42. That is, if you want to make $75,000, you're going to have to think and produce like a $75,000 person.

Time Is Money

Annual Income*	Each Hour Is Worth	Each Minute Is Worth	In One Year An Hour per Day Saved Is Worth
$10,000	$5.16	$.0864	$1,259
$20,000	$10.32	$.1723	$2,516
$30,000	$15.37	$.2551	$3,750
$40,000	$20.64	$.3596	$5,036
$50,000	$25.62	$.4268	$6,250
$75,000	$38.42	$.6400	$9,374
$100,000	$51.24	$.8536	$12,500

*Based on 244 working days of eight hours each.

Questions to ask yourself about your own time management and productivity:

- Do you finish important work first?
- Do you complete important tasks in a timely manner?
- Are the tasks you are doing contributing to reaching your goals?
- What tasks can you eliminate or delegate?
- Does a specific client or prospect deserve your time?
- Are you avoiding difficult tasks that could have a big impact on your success?
- Are you scheduling enough thinking time?
- Are you continuing your education and scheduling rest and relaxation time?

As I mentioned earlier, schedule some thinking time to

ponder what it is you are doing. Determine what things you should stop doing and what it is you are not doing now that you should be doing. Ask yourself the questions listed above the next time you set aside thinking time.

The Marine Corps has a philosophy summed up in the phrase, "First in, last out." I believe it also describes an attitude toward time management all professional sales people should adopt. Winners start early and stay late. They schedule breakfast meetings with customers and prospects to get more out of the day. "Last out" means the truly successful sales people do not quit early each day, even if they are discouraged. Moreover, they go the extra mile to satisfy their customers and impress their prospects. Wishing for more sales and higher income won't make it happen. It takes hard work, along with good planning and careful time management.

CHAPTER THREE

Be Prepared

Successful sales people do the things that unsuccessful sales people are too unwilling or lazy to do. If you are willing to train hard, make sacrifices and go the extra mile, you can be well on your way to achieving the success you crave. One's journey through life has an accumulative effect on its outcome. That means, everyday your actions are stacking up for or against your success and happiness. Over time, each tiny event, each individual effort adds up to massive amounts of change that propels you either upward to success or downward to disappointment. The key to selling success is consistency in doing the basics and executing with precision each and every selling maneuver. If you are consistent and also add a few trademark twists of your own to the process, more victories will come your way. To be a consistent winner, you must be prepared.

In the Kuwait War, we marveled at the precision with which the fighter pilots destroyed their targets with "smart missiles." Their performance was far from amateur's luck. Years of training, preparation, teamwork and commitment combined in an effort that allowed them to perform at their best when called upon to do so. All-star performers must continue to train and prepare to stay on top of their game. That includes sales people, too.

Learn About The Organization

Before visiting a potential client, remember the motto with five P's: "Prior Preparation Prevents Poor Performance." Before heading out on a mission, it is always best to scout around and gather intelligence. Then, prepare for the engagement.

Often you can find out many things about a potential client or customer just by reading trade magazines, newspapers and business weeklies. Go to the library, if necessary, and conduct a search for recent articles about the company. If the company is publicly traded, contact your broker and ask for copies of the annual reports.

Another method for gathering important information is to tap into a strong network of associates. I belong to two formalized groups known as leads or tips organizations. I consider these troopers my intelligence outfit. What's more, most members also are leaders in the communities in which they work and live. When I want to know something about a potential customer, someone in the group usually can get me the lowdown, either from first-hand experience, or from another knowledgeable source.

My network is comprised of bankers, accountants, lawyers, investment brokers, corporate insurance agents, and business advisors and consultants. If any member has a client that might benefit from my services, a recommendation and referral usually follows. If you do not already have a strategic coalition of five to ten associates, I would strongly urge you join an existing group or develop one. Behind every great campaign and every great leader is a team of top-notch advisors.

One of the most important things to find out about a

potential customer prior to a meeting is information about the company mold. That is, is the company culture or way of doing things conservative, progressive, open for change or stuck in very old patterns.

Find The Decision-Makers

It also helps to know who are the real decision makers in the company in advance of any encounter. When I opened my speaking and consulting practice, I first directed most of my marketing efforts to the directors of sales and the vice presidents of sales and marketing. I soon found out this approach was a mistake. That's because most often the CEO controls the purse strings of the sales department. Moreover, some sales directors and vice presidents thought it might be taken as a weakness on their part if they called in outside help to reinforce their effort.

In my corporate days I was, to some degree, a maverick. That is, I made decisions for such things as obtaining sales training for the sales staff without seeking prior approval. I assumed all managers did the same. I found out later that most individuals heading up sales departments in small to mid-sized firms cannot make many decisions without the approval of the CEO. Now, the target of my sales effort is the company CEO. My aim is better and so are my sales results.

When my associates cannot help me determine who are the real decision makers at a prospective company, I call a secretary or administrative assistant to ask for help. Once the decision maker is identified, you might ask the assistant the following question, "Can you help me by telling me what Mr./Ms. Big likes and dislikes in a sales representative?" You also might state something like, "I will be calling him/her for an appointment and I want to do my very best when we meet, so your help will really be appreciated." Most likely, the secretary or assistant will let Mr./Ms. Big know that you are a breath of fresh air and that you actually tried to do a little homework prior to your appointment. In addition, assistants are usually so flattered that someone is actually asking for their advice; they are often willing to help.

Be sure to drop an immediate note of appreciation to the person that helped you. A small box of candy or a flower in a bud vase might also be in order if the potential customer is a very big fish.

Get To Know The Troops

Prior to the visit or on the first call, try to get to know all of the supporting personnel. Can a secretary help you? Of course she can! Next question! Can a secretary hurt you? Of course she can! She can be your ally or your foe – it is up to you. The message here is to get to know everyone in the organization with which you hope to do business. Slight no one!

Bring A Benefit

Prepare to bring a benefit to the client on the first visit. Work very hard to present one new idea or concept that would interest or benefit the prospect or customer. Avoid at all costs making a visit that amounts to nothing but time wasted with useless talking. That's what most sales people do – lots of useless talking. When they finally get an appointment, they waste it with blabbering. If you do it too, you will soon find out how hard it is to get appointment number two. It's best to present an idea that has nothing to do with your products or services. For an example, if you see an article in a trade magazine or a newspaper that might be of interest to the client, clip it and be sure to bring it with you to present to the contact.

Another way to bring a benefit is to propose something that may be ordinary, but which you will accomplish it in an extraordinary manner. One way to do this is to find something to do personally for the client, something no one else has ever offered. For example, you might invite the prospect to join your customers at an event in which you engage a professional speaker to provide an interesting program. Do not talk about your products or services at the event. Just set up the event for fun, networking and business education. Let the outside speaker thank you for coming up with such a nice idea to bring "value and joy" to your clients and customers.

Another way to bring a benefit on the first visit is to ask the prospect, "What is the number one challenge in your company?" If, for example, the prospect replies, "improving the fuel mileage with our trucks," you could contact the State Department of Transportation to gather their research or visit a national trucking firm to see what they do to improve mileage. Then, present the findings to your prospect. Guess who will be the only sales person who asked the right question and acted on it to the benefit of the potential customer? To bring a benefit, become a problem solver and partner in success. Always look for benefits you can bring your customers beyond the limited benefits of your particular products and services.

Confirm The Appointment

When you finally land that important initial appointment with a potentially big customer, send a card or a short letter in advance to confirm the appointment. When doing so, mention the day, such as Thursday, the date and the time. I list both the day and the date because often people write down the wrong day on their calendars. It's also a good idea to send a card or a copy of the letter to the executive assistant, if appropriate, as further confirmation. This should always be done if it is an important call and you must invest considerable time and/or expense to meet the prospect. Many executives rely on their assistants to keep them on schedule. You should, too.

While doing a sales seminar in Lansing, Michigan, someone came up during a break to tell me about her brother. Her brother had a unique way of using the post office as a partner for getting appointments. He would routinely send notes in the mail to prospects. The notes read, "I want your business so bad I can taste it!" Along with the note, he enclosed a plastic fork. His persistence and imagination paid off and his ability to schedule appointments with key prospects improved significantly.

If we allow ourselves the freedom to use some creativity and be just a little different from everyone else, the appointments we are granted and the sales we make will increase. Most sales people make a very bland effort at getting an appointment, which is usually followed by a very bland meeting once the appointment is scheduled. Being creative often makes the client not only interested in seeing you, but in doing business with you.

Send Background Information In Advance

Send introductory information about you, your company, your services and how you believe you can benefit the company in advance of the appointment. By sending background information in advance, the sales person will not have to spend the appointment time trying to familiarize the prospect with his or her company. I always enclose reference letters and a credit application with the background information I send.

I include a credit application in advance because it smacks of confidence; confidence that I have something the client needs or wants and I can swing the deal. By enclosing a credit application, I send a signal to the client that I am very confident we will do business. In the introductory letter accompanying the background information, I usually add this P.S. "Would you please arrange to have the enclosed credit application completed so I can receive it on my arrival."

In the advance letter, explain exactly what you hope to accomplish during your visit. You might tell the prospect how much time you need for the meeting or ask the prospect to do one specific thing to get ready for your visit. For example, you might ask for information about the volumes of goods or services similar to yours they buy annually. A letter that attests to your professional approach to selling alerts the prospect and encourages him to also prepare to make the most of the possibilities involved in the forthcoming meeting.

List Objectives For Each Call

Prior to getting in the car or getting on an airplane, review each client/prospect file to determine exactly why you are going to see them. That is, what is the purpose of the sales call? What are you going to share? What benefits are you bringing? What do you hope to learn? List all the meeting objectives in order of importance and rehearse the outline to make sure it lends itself to an easy flow of conversation. If it doesn't, adjust your outline so one subject leads naturally to the next.

Things you probably want to find out about the prospect during the initial meeting include the following:

- From whom is the company now buying?
- What factors would make the prospect actively consider your products or services and your company?
- What will it take for you be worthy of the prospect's respect and business?

You also want to find out the prospect's credit worthiness immediately. You certainly do not want to waste time making a second or third visit to a prospect with a poor credit record.

Plan Your Travel

If you are driving in a new city or a new part of a town with which you are only somewhat familiar, be sure you know how to get to the scheduled appointment on time. If you are late, you already have one foot in the bucket! Often when people are in a hurry, they forget the obvious. Failure to plan your travel can cost you a sale.

If you are a member of AAA, call them and ask them to route

you from one appointment to the next. Let's say you are flying to Los Angeles and plan to spend two or three days making, 10 to 15 sales calls. Members can provide AAA with the different addresses, in the proper order and ask the AAA representative to send a "trip ticket." They will develop a packet, which will route the member from account to account. Often the trip tickets state the amount of time it takes to get from one call to the next.

If you are not a member of AAA, get a street map and route your travel as you set up appointments. Ask your clients or prospects for approximate travel time between locations.

That First Impression

You only have seven or eight seconds to make the first impression. Accordingly, you need to invest in clothing that will help you look your very best. Dress for the expectations of your customers. Know your customer type. Then, use your appearance to help inspire confidence and a willingness on the part of the prospect to develop a relationship with you and your company.

Match your clothing to the industry. The gentleman wearing a custom tailored suit when calling on ranchers or small business owners in rural America will only create instant suspicion and resentment. More casual dress is appropriate in this instance. Likewise, never dress casually when calling on corporate giants.

The best look for selling to corporate clients is a conservative one. For men, this means a dark suit. Navy, charcoal or black is best. The suit should be clean and well pressed. I recommend pinpoint cotton shirts. They cost a little more, but they look better, hold a press and last longer. You'll spend 25 percent more for a pin point shirt, but it should last two or three times longer than oxford cloth. I suggest you do not monogram your shirts on the cuff, and definitely not on the collar! Never wear something that might draw the prospect's attention away from your face. I have my shirts monogrammed a couple inches below the shirt pocket. The monogram will not show when I have on my suit jacket. The bottom of the tie should cover the belt buckle. I believe the best type of wristwatch is one that is understated. I also suggest men should not wear a wrist bracelet, unless they are in a city or industry, such as entertainment, where maybe it is chic to do so.

Women should consider investing in a session with an image consultant to select the most flattering colors and styles of business attire. Image consultants can advise women about the best colors for their skin tones. These consultants also can help women select the style of clothes to which they are best suited, and give advice regarding the use of cosmetics. Always dress in business attire when making a sales call. When in doubt, lean toward a conservative style and color. Women should always carry an extra pair of pantyhose in their glove compartment or briefcase. When you call on a client with a run in your stocking, you can guess what the client or prospect will be looking at!

My best advice is to be a little understated. By that I mean the only thing the prospect should say about your clothing is nothing. Prospects should, however, be impacted immediately by your professional look.

A clean, well-pressed outfit or suit from Sears will typically get a better response than a wrinkled, dirty, expensive one from I. Magnin. Polished shoes and proper fitting of hose and socks are absolutely necessary. Remember, a $75 tie will not be impressive if it is not tied to fit snugly around your neck and if it has a large stain from salad dressing on the front.

Ask one or two of your best friends or associates to advise you about what you can do to improve your appearance. Tell them you want to hear the truth about everything from your hairstyle and personal grooming to your clothing and shoes. If you do not look the part, you might be tuned out by the prospect before you get the opportunity to get involved in the selling process.

Clothing covers approximately 95 percent of the body. Since impressions are usually formed before the first word is spoken, it only makes good sense to look the part of a successful, professional sales or businessperson.

Your briefcase also gives the client or prospect an impression of you. It should be clean and neat inside and out. If the inside of your briefcase is messy, the prospect may question how well you would organize and handle his account. If the briefcase is dirty, tattered or badly worn, the client will assume that's the way you will take care of his order.

Would you close a $100,000 dollar contract with a plastic pen? On the other hand, would you close a $500 order with a very small client with a Mont Blanc® pen? Always carry both an inexpensive pen and an expensive one with you so you are prepared to make the right impression when doing the final paperwork.

Preparation Action Steps

For your first visit by remembering these action steps:

- Learn — Your first visit will be a learning experience for both parties. Prepare for the first visit by writing down the things you want to learn. Always remember that you want to ask targeted questions and then listen carefully to what is said. Listening inspires confidence. You would not want a doctor operating on your brain without asking a lot of questions. The axiom that is true for doctors is applicable to sales people - prescription without diagnosis is malpractice. Ask questions and listen in order to learn.

- Take Notes — During the visit, be conscious of the fact that every word that is spoken may be crucial. Taking excellent notes during the visit allows you to leave the client's office with information to study and re-study. This will help you discover big opportunities and little ones, as well.

- Discover — Explore for the specific things that might

cause clients to act or give you an order. They may be feeling ignored by their existing sales person or they may not even like the current sales representative. You can find out a great deal by always asking this question, "Mr. or Mrs. Client, if there is one thing that you would like your existing vendor to do better, what is it?" When the client responds to the first question you might follow up with another question such as, "Could you expand on that further?" Discovering what impacts the decision maker will help you structure a winning proposal.

- Interest — Mention the features of your product or service that are apt to interest the prospect most. Leave room for follow up.

- Deflect Objections — The average number of objections or reasons why the prospect will not buy is six. Besides price, what are the standard objections you hear most often? List the standard objections and rehearse answers to these objections that will make sense to the customer. In the future, when you hear these objections you can overcome them very smoothly with an appropriate response. View objections not as a personal rejection, but questions that must be addressed. It's always good to tell the client something like, "Great point-that's important." Then, address the concern.

You might remember during the 1984 presidential debate that Walter Mondale was placing his hopes for winning the debate and the election on the notion voters would reject President Reagan because of his age. Mondale constantly made reference to Reagan's age and also about how old he would be when he left office. Reagan's speech coach prepared him for this attack long before the televised debate with Mondale. Early in the debate, Mondale made the point about Reagan's age. For Reagan, it was like watching a baseball come floating over the plate in slow motion. He felt like the ball would never get there. When it did, Reagan didn't simply deflect the point, he hit it with everything he had by saying, "I am not going to make age an issue in this campaign. I am not going to exploit, for political purposes, my opponent's youth and inexperience." Do you remember that? Reagan went on to win the election!

Listen — Finally, prepare yourself to listen carefully in order to hear problems and opportunities. Generally, I find women listen better than men. Often, men listen to interrupt, while women listen to learn. Everyone can improve their listening skills. If you do not have targeted questions to ask and if you do not have good listening skills, your sales effort will suffer.

More on listening. Several years ago a management, consulting firm interviewed 432 corporate decision makers regarding the sales people that called on them. Some of the findings were as follows:

- 69% of all sales people were rated "fair to poor" by CEOs
- 49 % of salespeople talked too much
- 89 % of sales people did not ask the right questions

Nine out of ten sales people do not ask the proper questions which could uncover ways to satisfy a client. Again, almost half do too much talking. There are lessons to be learned from this study. First, it will take very little effort to be among the best sales people. Put bluntly, to be more successful at selling to executives, all it takes is to shut up, ask the right questions and spend your appointment listening to the customer.

Preparation is essential! Plan exactly how you want your first visit to proceed from the beginning to the end. Don't leave the meeting to chance. Take control of the opportunity by undertaking the necessary preparation.

In summary, be prepared:

- Do your homework, understand as much as possible about the prospect, the company and the support staff.
- Set the appointment and confirm it with some creativity.
- Gather your sales and presentations materials.
- Make careful travel arrangements and give yourself plenty of extra time to get to your appointment promptly.
- Dress properly to influence your prospect and help win approval.
- Prepare to listen, learn, discover opportunities, interest the prospect and take the first steps to developing a business relationship.

CHAPTER FOUR

Never Stop Prospecting

Never, never, never stop prospecting. Prospecting is the lifeblood of any organization with something to sell. "What you sow, so shall you reap," says the Proverb. In sales, that means the number of new customers you acquire is determined by the level of importance you give to prospecting.

Roger Wood Foods is a client of mine. The president of the company told me a story about the basic difference between a prospect and a customer. The story went like this:

> *A man had a bad automobile accident and lay dying in the intersection. An angel came down from heaven to give him the choice of going to heaven or hell. The dying man replied, "How do I choose? I don't know what either one is like. " He then was offered a two-day trip to visit both places. First, he visited hell. While there he saw people in bathing suits with tanned bodies, plenty of nice bars and restaurants, and a party atmosphere. Next, he made a trip to heaven and was unimpressed with everyone's low-key attitude and mundane dress. His decision was easy, he asked to go to hell. On his*

*arrival, he immediately smelted the foul odor of burning
flesh. Everyone was screaming from the pain of flames
that licked at their bodies and from the beatings they
endured. He called up to the angel with the question,
"Hey, what gives? " The angel replied, "When you first
visited hell, you were a prospect and they promised you
everything. Now, you're a customer."*

If you do not believe that a prospect will benefit by changing
suppliers and buying from you, and if you cannot deliver what
the customer expects, then you should not try to sell anything to
the prospect. Your reputation and that of your company depends
on promises kept. Never become "the vendor from hell." Your
reputation will spread and soon you'll be out of luck, if not out
of business. So, collect customers carefully.

One of the primary reasons for prospecting is because it's
essential to survival. The average life of a customer is only seven
years. Sooner or later, customers will quit doing business with
a particular vendor. According to the U.S. Small Business
Administration, customers evaporate because:

- 1% die
- 3% move away
- 5% move the business to friends or relatives
- 9% leave for competitive reasons
- 14% become dissatisfied with the product or service
- 68% change because the vendor has an indifferent
  attitude

Careful attention to customer service by everyone in the
company, and especially by the sales person, can dramatically
reduce the dropout rate. Often, I find people work very hard to
land a customer only to provide inadequate service following
the sale. Once you acquire a customer, you must dedicate
yourself to serving as an unpaid consultant to the client for the

life of the account. The minute you stop servicing the account and bringing new ideas and concepts to help the client, someone else, who is prospecting, will take your business.

Finding Prospects

Of all the sales people who terminate in their first year of selling, studies show that almost 80 percent of these unsuccessful individuals failed to do adequate prospecting. Therefore, to reach your goals, you must dedicate a reasonable amount of time each week to prospecting.

Newspapers and Trade Magazines

Newspapers and trade magazines can be a great resource. Read the daily and business newspapers in the territory you cover. I also suggest you subscribe to trade magazines in all appropriate related industries. The good news is most trade publications are free! Take these magazines with you to read on airplanes and even in the lobbies of customers. At present, I receive more than 200 trade magazines of which I'm only paying for two or three. I often find articles that would interest a particular client or prospect, even though the subject of the trade magazine is totally unrelated to the clients' industry.

Always read the business section of your local newspaper. It provides information about new companies coming to the area, new start-up companies, expansions, new product introductions and a whole host of other business issues. The newspaper is a valuable source for new prospects; read it and reap.

I always read the section where individuals are being recognized for their recent career promotion or professional achievement. Almost everyone considers a promotion a very important life event and almost everyone enjoys being recognized for his/her accomplishments. My personal, informal surveying has shown that when individuals are promoted, they receive an average of only two or three congratulatory notes from people in the business sector. If someone tells me they were promoted ten years ago and their name and photo was in a trade magazine or newspaper, I like to ask them how many sincere notes of congratulations they received. Then I ask if they can remember the names of the people who sent the congratulatory cards. Almost always, they can furnish the names! Sending a note of congratulations can help build relationships. These people might be prospects for your products or services; or, they could become members of your informal networking organization and supply you with leads and prospects in the future.

Another suggestion is to regularly read the help wanted classified section for prospects. Often, you will see corporations that could make excellent prospects advertising for employees. Secondly, you might see an ad for a production manager or a purchasing agent. You might know of an associate or contact who is interested in making a change in employment who might appreciate a job lead. You just might assist a friend gain employment in a key position with a future prospect of yours. Another good reason to read the help wanted section is to look for change. You might discover the purchasing manager at a company you have been unable to penetrate is finally gone by simply reading the advertisement for his position.

Trade Associations and Civic Organizations

Trade associations create numerous opportunities for prospecting. Prospects also can be found in organizations such as Sales & Marketing Executives, Jaycees, and Rotary. It's much easier to make appointments and to learn vital information about a company and its potential to become a customer in an informal atmosphere. Trade associations and civic organizations provide ample opportunity for the exchange of information at their various events.

At the very least, show up to meetings or attend association functions. Better yet, get into a position of leadership. Why sit in an audience at a trade convention and listen to one of your competitors give a speech? You need to be up there! Get involved in committee work. It leads to contacts. I have served as a volunteer on a Liberty Bowl and a Fiesta Bowl committee. In both cases, business from contacts I made during my service came very naturally. Giving time and personal service away to a non-profit association will eventually be rewarded. Join associations and organizations for which you have a passion and are interested in supporting. Don't worry about what you will immediately gain. What goes around, eventually comes around.

Trade Shows

If you exhibit at trade shows in order to display your products and interest new prospects in your offering, the following may serve as a helpful reminder:

- Develop a plan, which includes the purpose for exhibiting at the trade show, what you will exhibit, and how you will follow up.
- Be sure to have graphics, which tell people what you offer and the benefits provided by your products or services.
- Use the Marine Corps philosophy, be the first exhibitor to show up and the last one to leave.
- Keep everything in the exhibit area neat at all times.
- Have plenty of sales materials, but distribute them with discrimination.
- Be the best-dressed exhibitor.
- Never smoke in the booth.
- Have ample guest chairs, because people listen better when sitting.
- Place the back of visitor chairs next to the convention aisle to keep the prospect's eyes on you and not on people passing the booth.
- Take good notes on the interests of prospects. Use a form or write on the back of collected business cards.
- Carry company post cards with postage so that you can send a thank you note the very same day you met the prospect at the trade show.
- Qualify prospects at the show and prioritize for later

follow up.

Yellow Pages

The Yellow Pages Directory is a tremendous resource for prospects. Examine every major heading that remotely pertains to your industry. When I was in the food industry I learned quickly that if I just looked under the food heading in the Yellow Pages, I would be missing lots of prospects. I learned to look under headings such as bakers, canners, dairy, food manufacturing, food products, grocery distributors, health foods and other related headings. When you work a particular market, your object is to own it. So, think A-Z when you hit the Yellow Pages!

If your territory covers many cities, you also might get in the habit of looking under the section for associations. Often you can find small associations relating to your business that may be helpful to your effort. Find out when and where they hold their meetings and attend as a guest. Even if you do not find a prospective client, you may learn something that could be useful.

Get Referrals From Clients

Ask your existing customers for names of new prospects. Of course, it also is good business to ask for reference letters from your existing clients to keep in your file. My business would not be as strong as it is without reference letters and referrals from satisfied customers! Even when you conduct a prospect call or introductory visit, always ask who else you should be calling on that could benefit from your products and services.

Contact Associates In Allied Industries

Obtaining and developing a relationship with a group of associates in allied industries can be invaluable. Meet with them several times a year in order for you to exchange information. You may set up meetings in your office, or schedule breakfast or lunch meetings. Ask each participant to arrive with one solid sales lead for another party. After discussing how to support each other's efforts, you may ask a participant for a personal introduction to a prospect or to help you set up an appointment.

Good sales people always have more leads than they can handle. By reading, making friends, and always asking questions, you should never run out of leads.

Divide And Conquer

If your territory is a city, you should divide the city into at least four quadrants. For example, designate a northeast, southeast, southwest, and northwest quadrant. You may wish to assign two days in a particular week to prospect just one quadrant. Always carry your prospecting files with you, because sometimes you get in a particular sector of the city and have available time on your hands. You can then pull out your prospect file and call several prospective clients in that quadrant. Tell them how you came up with their name and let them know that you will be in their area, for example, all afternoon. Request a maximum of five minutes of their time to ask three or four questions, and assure them you will leave promptly at the five minute mark. Even if they do not have time to see you, you have at least made contact and you can determine if there is enough interest for follow-up.

Timing Is Everything

Timing is almost everything in sales. It is! So, you'll want to make your best impression on the first visit. Are you best in the morning or the afternoon? I often hear that some people are best in the morning. If so, they should start with breakfast appointments and schedule their most important visits before lunch. Personally, I find prospects seem to be most receptive on Tuesdays, Wednesdays and Thursdays. On Monday they are busy trying to get a lot of projects started and on Fridays they are trying to wrap up their week. Determine when you are at your best, in the morning or the afternoon. Then, schedule your appointments accordingly.

Abandon Fear

General William C. Westmoreland once said, "War is fear cloaked in courage." The thought of rejection strikes fear in the hearts of most sales people and sometimes paralyzes their courage.

Experts tell us most sales people do not do enough prospecting because they fear rejection. If fear is an emotion that hits home for you, try to view prospecting for what it is. It's the potential for creating additional income for the business and for the individual sales person. It's finding one more client that may need your products or services and help you reach your personal and business goals. It's also a numbers game — just that, a numbers game.

The one activity in the sales process that I get most excited about is prospecting! To me, prospecting for one entire week is exhilarating, because I understand selling is a numbers game. Of course, the quality of the prospects I contact is all-important. Even so, the best sales people know that you have to get a lot of turndowns in order to get a lot of orders. To succeed, you cannot be afraid of a prospect saying "no." Real fear comes from eating two bran muffins with four cups of coffee, then getting stuck in traffic. That's something to fear!

If you make a prospect call and it does not go well, do not toss away the information on the prospect and give up completely. Vendors go out of business or they lose their competitive edge. The prospect's needs may change or the buyer or purchasing agent may change. Change is constant. People are hired, promoted, demoted and fired. In addition, current suppliers could let them down. You may want to create a separate file for worthy prospects you may wish to re-contact in the future. Remember, nothing is forever.

Energize Your Effort

Whether your initial contact with a prospect is by phone, mail, or in person, show lots of high energy. Unfortunately, most sales people are boring. Their telephone conversations are boring and their business letters are mundane, at best. Speak with high energy on the telephone and display eagerness in person. Almost everyone wants to be around people with a positive outlook and those with charisma. Not everyone is born with charisma, but it can be developed. So, if you are not naturally loaded with it, just remember authentic charisma usually results from a lifetime of achievement. That means you cannot be charismatic and on top of your game by being good once in awhile. Being positive and enthusiastic consistently requires hard work and dedication over the long haul and hours invested in gaining the stamina necessary for prospecting and selling.

If you are on a roll and things are going well on any given day, get on the telephone and try to secure as many appointments as you can! On the other hand, if you are having a very bad day, you might decide to have someone call to cancel any key appointments. One way to handle this situation is to simply have an associate call the person and say, "John had an emergency come up and he will have to cancel his appointment." If you are having a bad day, it is an emergency! If you are having a bad day, the chances of presenting yourself in the best manner possible are slim. So, canceling the appointment might be a smart move. If you know you are going to lose a battle, don't be afraid to retreat and regroup. Save your effort until you have a superior advantage.

When you reschedule a cancelled appointment, you might be so bold as to tell the prospect, "To be honest, I cancelled the appointment because I was having one of those thoroughly rotten days and I only wanted to see you, Mr. Jones, when I was having a great day. If you were just an average customer, I would have come not at my best." That would be the truth and your statement would contain honest flattery.

On the other hand, if your appointment on that bad day was

with an accountant, you would not have to worry about your mood swing. Keep the appointment. I say this because most accountants only have one mood, and a major swing for them is like a small ripple on a horizontal line. Perhaps the observation is a bit exaggerated, but accountants typically are not sold by the sales person's enthusiasm. So, be prepared to show accountants lots of numbers and they will be happy, no matter what kind of mood you're in.

Follow Up Fast

Assuming that reading trade magazines and participating in association conventions, meetings and trade shows are effective methods for finding new prospects, it is important to follow up on new leads fast! Have you ever responded to an ad in a magazine asking you to circle a number and send in a response card for more information? Do you remember how long it took for the company to send the literature you requested? Often, it arrives so late you forgot you had asked for the information and probably are no longer interested in the product. Prompt response means immediately sending the literature and information requested. Then, strike again with a very timely follow-up call. Remember time is money. Send the sales material fast and call quickly before the interest wanes.

CHAPTER FIVE

Get An Attitude

This chapter covers the most essential ingredient for selling success, ATTITUDE. Who would follow a leader into battle, who said, "I don't think we can win this?" I would not and I bet you would not either. No doubt about it, enthusiasm sells and attitude is almost everything when it comes to sales success. But, it takes more than just a gung ho, positive thinking approach to gain the kind of attitude necessary to be great at sales.

Maybe you're thinking, "Attitude, that's just not me." If so, this chapter will help you determine if selling is what you should be doing with your life. All of us must be willing to change in order to grow — even be willing to fail if it provides the learning experience necessary to succeed in the future. It might even be necessary to symbolically try walking through walls in order to learn what works and what doesn't work. Trying new approaches is how one learns which adjustments to make to the effort. There is no magic formula for sales success. Each person brings his or her unique skills and personality traits to the process. What works for one, will not necessarily work for another. Your attitude about how you approach selling will determine just how successful you will be.

Flexibility and adaptability also are important. Today, the "good old boy" method of selling hardly works anywhere. Buyers are more sophisticated and they are looking for more sophistication and professionalism from people doing the selling. That means sales people must change or fall by the wayside. If you are not open to exploring change, you are doomed to struggle without achieving your full potential.

Be Open To Change

Change is difficult for most people. Nevertheless, I encourage you to embrace it. There is more change represented in the events described in today's newspaper than took place during the entire sixteenth century. I'm sure the day is coming when we will witness more change in one hour than people experienced in 100 years during the Middle Ages. Am I excited about that prospect? Not really. However, I know I must prepare to adapt to the circumstances and take the attitude that I can change the way I do things to meet the new expectations of my customers and potential customers.

I encourage you to embrace a philosophy that recognizes a changing world and sees change as opportunity. Be open to trying new approaches and adapting new lessons to the way you do things. Sometimes you may try an idea that simply does not work. That doesn't mean you should never try the idea again. You may need to fine-tune the idea so it does work, or use it under different circumstances.

Practice Brings Improvement

I doubt your first kiss was spectacular. I also doubt the first time you tried to parallel park you did it perfectly. I'm sure very few people hit a home run the first time they pick up a baseball bat. Likewise, I don't think most sales people are terrific at their first attempt at selling. In every instance, improvement comes with practice; and, practice requires discipline and a willingness to learn from others and keep trying.

Failure should be viewed as feedback, feedback that corrections are needed. Do not be afraid to fail today in order not to fail tomorrow. Handling failure or lack of success leads to growth and improvement. To change is difficult — not to change when necessary can be catastrophic to your business or sales career. Besides, trying new ways of doing things can keep you fresh, alive and excited. With solid basic sales techniques as a foundation, a little "nothing ventured, nothing gained" approach is always good advice.

Do Whatever It Takes

Early in my sales career, part of my territory included the state of Florida. I often stayed at a nice hotel so I could invite my clients to bring their families for a light supper and swim in the pool. I always invited the entire family, including the children. The parents enjoyed it because it was a night out. The kids could have a great time at the pool, and Mom did not have to cook. This gesture presented me as a "nice guy" who understood the pressures on modern families and was interested in clients as people, not just as customers.

Doing things for clients in a unique way can set you apart from your competitors. For example, offer to have a gourmet, French-style luncheon delivered to a prospect or customer you are having trouble reaching if they will schedule a brief appointment with you over the lunch hour. Many catering companies will gladly deliver and serve the meal. It's something new and the client probably will enjoy it. Moreover, your visit will take place during lunch at his office, so the prospect will feel he has no time to lose by seeing you.

Another idea is to offer an unusual incentive. For example, send a note saying, "I want your business so bad, if you place an order in the next 30 days, I will personally clean and wax your car free of charge." "Then, make arrangements for the new client and his family to spend a day at a local resort hotel to enjoy the facilities and give them a key to a room so they have changing and restroom facilities. While your new client is having a great time, you could be waxing his automobile. This idea might not fit your situation or your prospect's style. Nevertheless, it's an example of how to distinguish yourself from the rest of the troops. Just take the principle of the idea and creatively develop approaches of your own.

Handling Rejection

Again, selling is a numbers game. You must sift through lots of prospects to find a customer. You must be willing to brush off numerous objections and rejections to make a sale. How you handle rejection is an important part of your sales attitude.

The number of setbacks you encounter will definitely be greater than the number of victories you will experience. The more you do, the larger will be the number of both failures and victories. Failing to land an account or get an order is not fun. How you handle the setbacks will make the difference between ultimate success and failure. Develop a method for keeping rejection in perspective.

I believe one of the best ways to deal with rejection is to remember that the best way to handle falling off a bicycle is to get right back on it. The same applies to falling off a horse or striking out in a crucial baseball game. When faced with rejection, get back to selling as fast as you can.

I speak and consult for corporations and associations. I am the product. I can handle the rejection when another speaker or consultant is chosen instead of me. However, if I fail to obtain a 9.0 or a 10.0 rating after I deliver a speech, I do not absorb the rating well. I average about one speech every 18 months where the chemistry between the audience and me just did not click. The first time it happened, I was a wreck. I immediately shared the experience with two professional speakers who had been successfully speaking for about 20 years. They told me they also have had the same experience. That lessened the blow, but I found that the best way for me to overcome an average performance was to get back in front of a group as quickly as possible and get a whopping victory.

Babe Ruth, Mickey Mantle and Reggie Jackson had two distinctive aspects of their batting careers. All three struck out more times than their teammates and opponents. They also hit more home runs. For which of the two are they most remembered? The home runs, of course. Would not it have been a waste of talent if Babe Ruth or Hank Aaron struck out three times in a row and told their managers something like, "I just can't take this any more?"

You not only compete against other sales people, you also compete against yourself. Your competitors hope you will feel rejected and quit. If you give up, your competitors can win by default.

In the early 1990's, Cal Ripken of the Baltimore Orioles was closing in on Lou Gehrig's record for playing in the most consecutive games. Ripken was experiencing an off year. His numbers tumbled and the fans booed him. The press wrote articles suggesting Ripken stop chasing Gehrig's record and take a break.

None of his critics understood Cal Ripken. He loved his profession and he looked forward to playing every day. Headaches, fatigue and a critical press never stopped him from getting out there, day in and day out, to take his swings. The next year he won the Most Valuable Player award for both the All-Star game and for his league!

At 22 years of age, I was about to join a Fortune 100 Corporation and I was told by a friend I could expect to be treated like a number. When I was 24, I entered the industrial sales field and was told by my regional manager that I was "too young and inexperienced" to be successful. When I was 33, I applied for a Vice President of Sales and Marketing position and

I was initially told I was about "10 to 15 years too young" for the job. I did well in all three positions. I am glad that I did not listen to those who had nothing to offer but negative comments.

Never Discount Luck

Luck is certainly part of the success equation in sales. Believe that luck is possible and you'll be lucky. Good things happen to people who are open to receiving them. Furthermore, luck is almost always earned. If I'm interviewing someone for a job and she tells me she does not believe in luck, her chances of being hired are diminished. People with the right sales attitude are smart enough to know luck plays a significant role in success. They also know they have a great deal to do with having luck come their way.

Bad Attitudes Are Bad For Business And Your Health

A bad attitude can do much more harm to us than we once thought possible. For years, the medical profession led us to believe most Type A personalities would die early. You know the sort, the overachieving workaholic always on the go. On-going research showed, however, that it was not every Type A personality who dies young, only those who have a constantly angry attitude. That's an important distinction. It's not the hard-driving individual trying to grab for the gusto who experiences early health problems. It's the hard-driving jerk who cannot channel anger and disappointment that drops dead early, usually to the relief of those around him or her.

I firmly believe you can enhance all your other skills and your health by keeping a positive attitude. Part of a positive attitude is a good sense of humor. Even when you are going through criticism and rejection, you can use humor to dispel their negative effects. If your boss jumps on you for some action, use a line such as, "I didn't do it and I'll never do it again." Or you might state with a smile, "Is there anything else you don't like — I'm on a roll here." This type of attitude helps you to absorb and redirect someone's anger and paves the way for re-establishing the relationship.

The Can Do Attitude

Winners often stand alone. Their "can do" attitude sets them apart. When you achieve success and reach the top 2 percent of your field, you must be prepared to leave some of your friends and associates behind. While you will be growing and prospering, they will be languishing behind, envying your success rather than making the changes necessary for them to succeed, too!

As a general rule, success is comprised of 15 percent aptitude (ability) and 85 percent attitude. A sales person, with an average or less than average positive attitude, stands very little chance of competing successfully for an order against someone with a great attitude. You might have six years of higher education under your belt, several years of experience and extraordinary product knowledge. Yet, if the competitor's attitude and willingness to do whatever it takes to please the customer is greater than yours, your competitor will almost always win — even if his credentials are not as impressive as yours. Credentials may help you get the job, but from day one, it's performance that counts. Performance is directly related to the performer's attitude.

Bounce Back, Bounce Up

I am a realist. I understand how difficult it is to remain upbeat all the time. Each of us experience bad days, days when even the M & M's melt in our hands. It happens to everyone in sales. When you're having a bad day, don't be afraid to acknowledge it. If it helps, talk it over immediately with a boss, confidant or friend. Talk to the right person, one who will listen and understand you. Make sure the person you confide in will give you quality feedback and will help you get going again.

How long does it take to bounce back from rejection and disappointment? The time varies from person to person. If it takes you a day to bounce back, try to reduce the recovery time to one-half of a day. If it takes you one-half of a day, work on bouncing back in one hour. In every situation, try to get any feelings of rejection, anger or disappointment out of your system before you go to bed. If you go to bed in a bad mood, you will almost always wake up the next morning in a bad mood.

Find A Coach, Not A Couch

Role models and mentors will help you advance quicker. Pick one that is very successful in business or sales and befriend him or her before asking for help. The real winners are almost always glad to help and usually are interested in the success of others. Winners are like thermostats — they set the temperature. Losers are like thermometers — they go up and down according to the conditions. Pick someone who acts like a thermostat.

If you invite your role model to join you for breakfast or lunch, always pick up the check. You should treat the role model like a client. The information and advice you'll receive will be worth much more than the cost of the meal. You should never ask a mentor to lunch, pick his brain and stick him with the check. NEVER.

Learn the birthday, anniversaries and special preferences of your role model so you can use the occasion and information to acknowledge the individual's importance to you from time to time. In other words, don't just take from your role models, make it a mutually beneficial relationship. Ask yourself, "With whom am I hanging around and what are they doing to me?" Charlie Brown, the cartoon character, is portrayed as a loser. He hangs around with Lucy! She's the one who gets him into trouble and sets up his failure. Don't pick a Lucy for a mentor.

Work On Your Attitude

Invest in motivational books, tapes, and seminars. Never ask how much is the cost of an audiotape or book. Rather, ask yourself, "How much will these tapes be worth to me?" Remember, the book you do not read cannot help you. It's amazing that 90 percent of books and audiotapes available on the topic of sales are bought by only ten percent of all sales people. Guess which ten percent are the buyers? The winners are the successful ones who understand they must keep learning new things to stay on top. Try to work harder on improving yourself. Working harder on yourself will ultimately lead to bringing more value to your employer, your clients or your business.

Take An Attitude Check

Understanding your strengths and weaknesses will enable you to capitalize on your strengths and take steps to eliminate weaknesses. No one is perfect! Successful people, however, do something about their shortcomings. If you lack good communication skills, take college courses or hire a consultant to provide individual coaching. If your wardrobe is not enhancing your image, make the investment in a nicer wardrobe. Few weaknesses are insurmountable. Whatever the weakness, resolve to take action to minimize or eliminate any barriers to your success.

Golda Meir, the former prime minister of Israel, commented once that she knew early in life she would never be pretty. She felt that realization was a blessing because it made her develop other talents and abilities. If your sales effort is hampered by your company's higher prices, for example, figure out how to personally bring more value to the customer to justify the higher cost. In other words, compensate in other ways for things that might make selling a challenge and the things that you may not be able to control. All sales representatives start out inexperienced. All corporations start out very small. Both begin without many strengths and loaded with many weaknesses. Just as successful individuals and corporations overcome many adversities to succeed, so can you. It's a matter of attitude, the willingness to change and to try different approaches and the resiliency to bounce back from disappointment.

Spend time and effort working on your individual winning attitude. Yogi Berra pointed out (as only Yogi can) the importance of the mental game by saying, "Baseball is 90 percent physical and the other half is mental." His percentages may not add up to 100 percent, but his understanding of how the mental process impacts the success of any endeavor couldn't be more accurate. Think hard about how you can develop a consistent winning attitude.

Here's a few points about failure, points I learned from my pastor. Failure is never to be feared because:

- Failure can educate us,
- Failure can identify skills that need development,
- Failure helps us discover our best talents,
- Failure makes us less judgmental of others, more tolerant,
- Failure is merely a setback, not a final outcome.

Is my pastor a motivator and coach? You bet! Can I learn something from a pastor, from a mailman or from a waitress? Absolutely! We can learn something from almost everyone in this world. The key to success is to hang around the right people, those that have the right attitude and can help you develop and maintain a successful attitude of your own.

CHAPTER SIX

Make The First Call Count

Never forget the objective of your mission. Your mission is to find and keep more customers. If you do that, profits and higher income will naturally follow. Getting more customers starts with prospecting, then making contact so you can get that first important appointment or telephone interview. If your business depends on personal visits to prospective customers to generate a sale, making your first in-person call count is paramount.

Get Attention

Here's a sure fire way to get attention. When the prospect or customer tells you to come any time between 8:00 AM and 11:00 AM next Tuesday, ask for an 8:03 appointment. How often does someone ask for an 8:03 appointment? Never! You instantly leave an impression with the prospect that you are different.

Immediately send a post card or a confirming letter stating you will arrive at 7:59 AM for your 8:03 AM appointment. Now you are really different! Where do you think the prospect will be when you arrive? Many times, he or she will be in the lobby looking at their watches to see what time you arrive. Frankly, they also are curious to see who is this "screwball." That's OK. You have a choice. Do you want to plug along like the typical sales person with a typical approach to sales calls, or do you want to try to set yourself apart from the pack at the very beginning of the race? You should choose an approach that's comfortable, but I vote for being different right out of the chute.

If you are trying to set up an appointment that would take place over a meal, I recommend breakfast meetings instead of lunch meetings. I like breakfast meetings because they significantly increase my productivity. Moreover, they generally are more focused and shorter than lunch and dinner meetings. More is accomplished in a shorter period of time. Just think, if you scheduled a breakfast meeting for every Monday through Friday for one complete year you would have scheduled 250 extra appointments before 8 AM! Breakfast also is a good time for a sales meeting because the customer is fresh and not distracted by things going on at the office or shop.

Meal Meetings

For meal meetings to be successful they must be carefully staged, employing precise tactics. If your territory is a city, divide the city into four quadrants and make the effort to find the best breakfast or lunch restaurant in all four quadrants. Frequent each restaurant on a regular basis, so the restaurant staff will become familiar with you. Become well known to the owner, manager or hostess as well as several members of the serving staff.

The day before the first important meal appointment, call the restaurant and tell them you would like to make a reservation for a specific time and that you would like to have a table away from swinging doors, noises, and other distractions. If the appointment is going to be a crucial meeting, you might even go to the restaurant the day before to brief the manager and waiter. The following is an example of what you might say:

Tomorrow I have a meeting with Ms. Jones. I have written all of this down for you, but I would like to just take two minutes of your time to ask for your help. I would like you to greet Ms. Jones by name and automatically pour hot tea for her. She doesn't drink coffee, so, just greet her by name, escort her to the table, pour hot tea and then leave us alone for a few minutes.

Now, I would like you to take my credit card, imprint a charge slip and give the card back to me. That way, when Ms. Jones and I feel that it is time to leave tomorrow, we can get up and leave without delay. Put an automatic 30 percent tip on my credit card slip, which I will pre-sign. Tomorrow mail my copy in this stamped, self-addressed envelope. As you continue to take good care of me and my clients, and make me look good, I am known to tip as much as 50 percent.

Do you think I get a waiter's attention when I pay a 30 percent tip and often as much as 50 percent? You bet! If you do not tip up front, the waiter or waitress will assume that you are going to leave a 10 or 15 percent tip. Remember what tips stands for. "Tips" is an acronym for "to insure prompt service." Consider this, what is the difference between a 15 percent and 30 percent tip on two breakfasts? Not much! Also, how many times do you think a waiter or waitress has been given a 30 percent tip? I have yet to meet an accountant who disagreed with the idea of a 30 percent tip, or more, for a great breakfast meeting. Such tipping might cost more for lunch or dinner meetings; but depending on the customer, it could be well worth it if you can get the kind of impressive service that will favorably impact the customer and help close the sale.

The best reason for pre-signing your credit card voucher is to enable you to get up and leave the restaurant whenever it is convenient for both you and the client. All of us have experienced how a damper can be placed on an otherwise successful event because the waiter or waitress would not bring a timely check. By paying in advance and stating the tip amount in advance, you can leave when it suits you. Believe me, your service level will be extremely high when you tip in advance. If you cannot make these arrangements in advance by arriving early or stopping by the day before, excuse yourself during the beginning of the meeting and take care of the check and tip while your guest thinks you are in the restroom.

To add impact to the meeting, as you leave hand the client a folder containing literature in which you have highlighted two or three significant things that correspond to what you discussed at the meeting. Also include a thank you note, which might state, "Thank you for joining me for breakfast and helping to get my day off to such a great start. Sincerely." You also might include a small box of gourmet candies or chocolates. Do you really care if Ms. Jones, her assistant, or someone from her family gets the chocolates? No! It's the thought that counts. Your client will be thinking about your preparation for the meeting and your thoughtfulness.

Again, Advanced Preparation is Essential

Whether you are meeting a customer at a restaurant or at the customer's office, preparation is essential. Get your clothes laid out the night before so you are not rushed in the morning. If it is an important call, dress to look your best. For most situations, men should wear a dark suit and women should have conservative attire in colors that enhance their appearance. Always make sure shoes are polished. Business cards should be impeccable, as well as the presentation materials you will use. In the event your client will ride in your automobile, it must be spotless. Even if you do every other thing correctly, escorting a prospect in a car that is dirty on the inside is a deal killer.

Lasting impressions are often made before the first word is spoken. Your car, your clothing, your shoes, your business card and anything else that will accompany you to an appointment will create a favorable or unfavorable impression — instantly.

Men should remove pens from their shirt pockets and place them on the inside of their coat jackets where they will not be seen. Again, carry two pens – an inexpensive one and an expensive one. If the client uses a BIC®, you do not want to pull out your Mont Blanc®.

If you have not called on a particular client before, be sure to allow plenty of time to get to the appointment promptly. If necessary, drive to the location the day before to learn your way around local streets and understand traffic patterns. Few soldiers want to go into battle without the benefit of advance scouting and reconnaissance.

Visit the prospect's office in advance or talk to an assistant by telephone to learn as much as possible about the person you will be meeting. Try to determine the decision-maker's personality type. Are they analytical? If so, be prepared to give facts and figures and the impact on the bottom line. If they are an entrepreneurial type, get to the point quickly and leave on time. If they are security conscious, be prepared to provide them with reassurance. In the last case, it might be smart to suggest a two-person meeting, so a collective decision can be made. The point, ask someone in the company prior to your appointment how the prospect can be approached best.

Getting to the appointment on time allows you a few moments to utilize the restroom to check your hair, tie or makeup, and to make sure that every part of your attire is in place. Remember not to sit on your jacket while driving the car. The last thing the prospect will see when you leave the appointment is the back of your jacket. Sometimes they will notice the back of your shoes so remember to keep liquid shoe polish handy for last minute touch ups.

Some "self talk" as you're walking in will prepare you mentally for the encounter. Walk briskly and start repeating to yourself, "I am going to knock them out with this presentation," or "I'm really going to bring these people tons of value." Remember prospects will be thinking one of two things immediately. Either, "I'm really going to like this person," or "I wonder how long this meeting is going to last?" Prospects will pick one of those thoughts in the first seven seconds, which means you should be prepared to approach them in a style they will instantly like.

An associate of mine scheduled an appointment with a woman at my office. The associate told me, "Bill, you are really going to like this lady." When I asked her why, she said, "This lady was very energetic on the telephone." I said, "Let's get a cup of coffee 15 to 20 minutes before her arrival, so we can watch her walk across the parking lot. I will then let you know if your assessment of her is correct." The lady arrived, got out of her car and proceeded across the parking lot toward the front door as if she meant business! The tone for the meeting was already set. And, my associate was right; I did like this lady. When you walk in, look the part. That is, act like you mean business and be eager. Shake hands like you mean it. When asked how you are, respond with "great" not "fine." Take a little time for personal conversation, but get down to business right away.

Remember, you have only seven seconds to make the right first impression. You will be sized up by the following criteria:
- 55% by the way you look.
- 38% by the way you present yourself.
- 7% by what you actually say.

Think about that! Ninety-three percent of a prospect's opinion of you will be based on the way you look and your personal style. That means you must look sharp and use every ounce of charisma you have to make a favorable impression. Doing lots of talking won't make the sale.

Show Respect And Enthusiasm

Always be sure to use "yes, sir" or "no, ma'am" at least once or twice during the conversation to show respect for the person you are meeting. You should not place any of your materials on this prospect's desk without asking. Smart people do not throw or slide their business cards and literature across the desk. Always treat your materials with loving care and respect, personally hand them to the prospect at the appropriate time.

If you are not naturally charismatic, show excitement and enthusiasm. Almost everyone is operating under stress. That gives you the opportunity to be the bright spot in the prospect's day. Be sure to use words such as "profit," "cost reduction," "service" and "save" in your conversation. Most importantly, do not to talk too much about your products and services on the first visit. Position yourself as a problem solver. That calls for asking many questions so you can come back for a second visit with suggested solutions. Do not be in a rush to open your briefcase. Rather, after a few personal comments, begin with your first question. Always include the word "you" in your discussion.

One of the most persuasive discussions I ever made included the word "you." The Baltimore Orioles were playing their initial season at their new baseball park, Camden Yards, in the early 1990's. They were experiencing one sell-out crowd after another and tickets were very hard to get. I decided, however, that I would go to the stadium, stand in line and hope to get tickets for my son and me. I was thinking positively, when I told my son to fly to Baltimore from Phoenix so I could take him to the brand new ballpark. I told him I was sure, one way or another, that I could get tickets.

I stood in a long line, proceeding very slowly toward the ticket booth. Then, the worst happened. One gentleman wanted to exchange tickets for 16 games! That transaction alone took about 15 or 20 minutes. The next man stepped up to the window in a foul mood, after having to wait so long. The ticket vendor, who was all of 18 or 19 years old, told the gentleman he could not help him because he was in the wrong line. The man went ballistic on the poor kid, then stormed away.

Being next in line, I stepped up to the window and told the

flustered teenager that I wanted three tickets. I said, "I would like to get three tickets for tomorrow night's game and I would like to get the best tickets available. One is for me, one is for my son who is about your age and is flying in from Arizona for the game and the third ticket is for you." He left the window, came back with three tickets and said, "Sir, you are going to love these seats. They are right on top of the first base dugout." I am confident that my attitude and the word "you" got me those tickets! When everyone benefits from a transaction, it's easy to make the sale.

Establish Yourself As A Professional

From the beginning, you must establish yourself as a professional if you want to be successful at selling. Be knowledgeable about your products and services and knowledgeable about the company on which you are calling. You will not be able to state the one benefit that will be the key to making the sale until you have asked all the right questions. Remember, do not talk about your company or your products - talk about the prospect's company and it's needs. Try to identify at least one crucial benefit that differentiates your offering from those of your competitors. This benefit must add to the buyer's security, reduce headaches, bring opportunities or increase profits for the individual making the purchasing decision and for the company. You must concentrate on the buyer's benefits because almost every customer is thinking only about what advantages will be gained by any relationship. Professionals know that no company will have a long-term competitive advantage by stressing only their products, services or price. So, top-notch sales professionals are always working on ways to bring added value to the customer and build relationships.

If you are not able to find out in advance of the appointment who the prospect is currently doing business with, find out during your first visit. Be knowledgeable about your major competitors. Develop a chart to give you a simple overview. First, list across the top the most significant factors involved in the purchasing decisions in your industry. Then, list your competitors along the side, placing X's for a competitor's strength and 0's for a weakness.

In the example following, if you were competing against Company B the one thing you would not want to stress is price, because Company B sells on price, but delivers poor service and less quality. Preparing a comparison chart of your own will enable you to determine what you will emphasize to the prospect and what factors you will not bring into the presentation.

Analysis Of Competitor's Selling Advantages And Disadvantages

Competition	Representative	Price	Service	Quality
Company A	X	O	X	X
Company B	X	X	O	O
Company C	O	O	X	X
Your Company	X	O	X	X

On the first visit, determine if the person you are calling on is the sole decision maker. Sales representatives have been known to call on one person endlessly only to find out their contact did not have decision making power. Ask who else is involved with making purchasing decisions and ask if you can meet with them. No one can sell your products as enthusiastically as you can. Therefore, the last thing you want is someone else trying to sell your products or services within the company. Call on people involved in the decision, even if it means a second visit and inconvenience for you.

Successful selling requires preparation and knowledge. Have in your mind or at your finger tips complete information about your products and services and all their benefits, your competition and their strengths and weaknesses and background information on the prospect's company. You will elevate your chances for closing a deal if you present yourself as knowledgeable and thorough.

Visual Aids

Visual aids, utilized properly, increase sales. Visual aids can have more impact on the customer than your verbal message. Actually, printed materials are 15 times more powerful than spoken words! Typically, people have an attention span of only three sentences. If you do too much talking, your presentation will go in one ear and out the other.

In a typical conversation, most people speak at a rate of approximately 150 words per minute. That number contrasts greatly with the rate at which we hear and think. People think at a rate of 400 to 500 words per minute. Prospects thinking patterns are often way ahead of the salesperson's presentation, and they could be thinking about things other than what is being said by the salesperson.

There are many advantages to utilizing visual aids. Among the most important:

- Presenters are perceived as more professional when they use visual aids.
- Visual aids add credibility and clarity to a presentation.
- Visual aids generate more interest from the viewer.
- Visual aids can present information creatively.
- Visual aids present facts more persuasively.
- Presentations are more dynamic and organized with visuals aids.
- People are 43% more likely to be persuaded when visual aids are used.
- Visual aids can reduce the time necessary for a presentation by 40%.

If you are making a sales presentation to a large group,

consider developing excellent visual aids. I always utilize a generous number of colorful slides or overheads. Without the slides or overheads, a visual imprint to reinforce the information has not been made in the brain. I try to personalize each presentation by developing some customized slides specifically for a particular audience. When the first customized slide is shown, the group knows that I have done my homework and I instantly get their attention.

I often ask members of an audience to raise their hands if they have thought of something other than the topic of the meeting while I have been speaking. I let them know that they will not hurt my feelings by raising their hands. I always see 50 to 75 percent of the hands go up. That is proof positive that if I just did a lot of talking to a group without using visual aids and asking lots of questions, their attention would drift.

For one-on-one presentations, elaborate visual aids are not necessary. A folder with company brochures and graphics on 8½" x 11" paper to reinforce product benefits or key sales points will do nicely. Present each page of materials when you are discussing the topic. If you hand the prospect the entire package, he or she will probably thumb through it as you are talking and not hear a word you are saying. Again, visual aids work best when they reinforce visually what you are saying.

Express Confidence

Making eye contact is critical. Muggers on the street usually decide they will mug someone by looking at the eyes and walking style of potential victims. Typically, if you look confident and determined, muggers will leave you alone. In hand-to-hand combat, I believe that looking mean and screaming causes many opponents to lose courage. Body language sends strong messages. Not looking someone straight on sends a message that you are not being genuine or sincere, or that you have a tremendous amount of insecurity and lack of confidence in your products and abilities.

Take Notes

Always ask permission to take notes. Requesting permission accomplishes two things. First it makes the note taking seem less threatening. Second, it shows most people that you are business like and you will follow up because you are careful about taking good notes. This establishes confidence in you and your company on the part of the prospect.

Unsuccessful sales people often drop the ball. They do not do what they say they will during a contact with a customer or client. Without notes, you will retain only a very small portion of the conversation. Listen carefully and jot down every detail. That's because as you proceed with the prospect, how you handle one of the small details could make or break a deal. A long pencil is much better than a short memory.

Pay Attention To The Little Things

Taking care of the little things often can pave the way to an easier closing. Ignoring the little things can blow a deal right out of the water. The way you handle the small details will determine the course of events and whether or not you'll walk away with a purchase order.

You might remember a disaster the United States Army experienced in Somalia in 1993. They hurriedly sent a group of Rangers, Special Forces of highly trained soldiers skilled in every type of warfare except urban encounters, to a hotel to capture General Aidid's aides. They were sent on the mission without the support of tanks and armored personnel carriers. The soldiers ran into an ambush and because the Secretary of Defense had denied a request for tanks and APC'S, the soldiers were trapped and picked off one at a time. The moral of the story is to plan explicitly how your mission is going to go, get sufficient support and make sure you're trained to fight on someone else's territory. Take care of the details before, during and after the encounter.

I think it is worth repeating the following routine. No later than the night before you see a client, prepare an outline of all of the things that you want to share and learn. Again, the outline should flow logically from one topic to another. That is, one question or comment should lead to the next one. If the outline does not have a good flow, rearrange it until it does. Make sure you have all your materials and complete knowledge of your product and your competition. Prepare, prepare, prepare!

I always encourage sales people to be different from the colleagues they compete against. The consensus of opinion in the business community is most sales representatives are boring! Always come with a fresh idea or a benefit for the buyer and the buyer's organization. If you make a call on the same customer every month, come with an eagerness to learn something and provide something of real benefit in return. Don't waste time making a contact or sales call if you do not have specific objectives to accomplish.

Don't Be Boring

Even a dull industry can be exciting. Not too long ago I saw the advertising slogan of a sanitation company printed on a company truck. The slogan read, "We're number one in the number two business." Now, you may not love that slogan, but it is different and it is an attention grabber! That company has tried to pump some pride, enthusiasm and even a little humor into its approach to doing business.

Look For Patterns

Examine your three best sales visits. Determine the common characteristics of these visits. You may find your best calls occurred on a certain day of the week or always in the afternoon. I make my best sales visits when I have on one of my favorite custom-made suits. A custom suit, a custom shirt and one of my favorite ties sends a message to my brain that I am really going to be "on." If you want to be boring, go into the oil drilling business. If you do not want to be boring, concentrate very hard on bringing joy and value to your customers with each and every contact.

It Takes Personality

The personality you display on a sales visit will influence the purchasing decision more than your products or services. The primary reason people switch vendors is because a decision is made about individuals. Buyers ask, "With which person would I rather do business?" People often think, "I really like this person and I really want to help him/her to succeed." Of course, successful sales people also must have products and services of quality and value to sell. Nevertheless, getting people emotionally involved with the sales process can move mountains. In most cases, people buy based on emotions, then justify their decision with logical reasoning. People love to buy from people they like; sales people who love to sell.

Use Body Language

When visiting clients lean forward in your chair. This expresses extreme interest and eagerness. I often will lean forward with my left forearm on my left knee as it shows that I am listening hard. I also raise my right hand to place a finger or two on my chin or cheek which shows that I am thinking about what they are saying. Study body language and use the knowledge to your advantage. While you are out selling, you may call on some individuals who are insecure or will feel intimidated when meeting with you. If they fold their arms and take a defense posture, try to hand them something immediately so that they will have to unfold their arms to receive what you are handing them. If you can get them to unfold their arms, you usually can get them to unfold their minds. Understanding body language is important to successful selling. If this is an area where you could use some additional information, read a book on the subject or take a course at a local college.

Engage The Prospect

Always try to get the prospect to do something for you. For example, ask for their help. I frequently ask the prospect if we can walk to get a soft drink or a cup of coffee. That gets the prospect in the habit of doing a few things to help or to satisfy me, and provides an opportunity to chat about personal topics. Rarely will a prospect turn down a simple request. When was the last time you asked someone for their help and they gave you a very blunt "no!" No matter where I've conducted business nationally or internationally, I've found most people are nice, professional and accommodating. People are most apt to respond favorably when you are nice, accommodating and professional, too.

Before ending the first meeting, summarize the discussion, stating what each has agreed to do as follow up. If you have not already acquired their credit information, try to get a credit application completed prior to your departure. Often customers order ahead of schedule, or at the last minute imposing tough deadlines. When an organization gets an order from a company without a credit check on file, the accounting department – I kiddingly refer to them as the customer prevention department – often will hold the order until all of the appropriate credit information has been gathered. If the customer needs an immediate shipment and the accounting department holds up the process, the customer you have worked so hard to obtain may leave you prior to ever receiving the first order. The best sales professionals anticipate problems and do everything necessary to avoid them in the first place. They know gathering credit data is crucial. First, they do not want to make a second visit to a company that has a poor credit rating. Second, if they know the client will be ordering eventually, the process will be easier if credit information can be obtained on the first visit.

Exit With Grace

Timing again comes into play when making your exit from the meeting. Leave before the appointment time is up and never over stay your welcome. Often people ask for just five or ten minutes, then stay for 30 or 45 minutes. Such behavior makes it very hard for the sales person to get a second appointment. Offer to leave at the time you promised to do so. If your visit is bringing tons of joy and value, the client may ask you to stay longer to complete your mission. Be smart and be prepared to leave five minutes before you promised.

Begin Follow-Up Immediately

Drop a post card m the mail to the prospect the same day you made your first visit. It can be just a short note to thank the client for the visit and to let him/her know you will follow up as promised. Then, immediately complete the follow-up steps you promised to do in the meeting. If it's important to make an impression, send your follow-up information and samples by courier or priority mail.

In summary:

- Do your homework thoroughly.
- Dress yourself for a positive first impression.
- Be a good listener; understand the needs of the prospect.
- Use your personality to gain rapport.
- Take detailed notes.
- Never over stay your scheduled time.
- Try to get credit information on the first visit.
- Follow up immediately.

CHAPTER SEVEN

Build Relationships

In the military, respect is earned by performing well under pressure and by being a responsible leader. Leadership gets things done. Great military officers understand that gaining a victory by unnecessarily sacrificing the lives of their soldiers is stupid. Morale suffers and results are poor when people perceive their leaders are not looking out for their best interests.

There is a lesson here. Never do things merely for personal gain, especially if it is at the expense of others. Long-term success means building trust. All things being equal, most customers prefer buying from sales people who treat them with respect and in whom they trust. Having a friendly, thoughtful personality is not enough. The company you represent must be capable of delivering the goods! You may be able to win a few orders on the strength of a pleasing personality, but after awhile customers will demand performance from you and your company. You'd better be ready to deliver.

Many years ago I read an article about the Jimmy Dean Sausage Company in a food industry magazine. In the article, Jimmy Dean shared many of his philosophies about his employees and his quality products. I wrote a letter to Mr. Dean telling him how much I appreciated his business convictions and I stated that the philosophies of our two companies were almost identical.

At that point in my career, I was serving as vice president of sales and marketing for a modest-sized ingredient firm. Landing an account with the Jimmy Dean Company would do wonders not only for our bottom line, but also for the morale of our entire organization. In my letter to Mr. Dean, I suggested both of our firms could benefit from a business relationship. He sent a letter back inviting me to come to Dallas for a visit. Prior to departing for his Dallas headquarters, I posted his letter on the bulletin board to get the workforce excited about the type of clientele we were approaching.

The local sales representative and I were met at the Jimmy Dean headquarters with all due courtesy. I left the visit excited by our meeting and the future possibility of turning them into a customer. Two weeks passed and I had not heard from our sales person regarding his progress with the sausage company. So, I called him. I asked, "How are you doing with the Jimmy Dean account?" His reply, "Bill, I went back there two times and I was told that I was wasting my time." My question back to our sales person was, "Tell me all the value added ideas and concepts you delivered on those two visits." He replied, "I guess I delivered none." I said, "Then, they didn't mean you were wasting your time; they meant you were wasting their time." When you're dealing with a very large and progressive organization, just showing up does not cut it.

Today, business is very competitive and very tough. Organizations are running lean and managers are working harder for less reward. Showing up with a box of donuts might be nice, but showing up with ideas or information to help the business and the contact succeed has far more impact.

To salvage the effort, I asked the sales representative to

contact the best French bakery in Dallas and place an order for several dozen pastries for us to take to Jimmy Dean's offices. We walked in and offered the first pastry to the receptionist. Then we asked that she call all of the secretaries and assistants to come up and get a pastry of their choice and also take one to the person to whom they reported. There was no doubt that within just a few minutes, every support person knew who we were and thought well of us. With this little offering, we had at least made a dent in the armor.

One of the ladies commented that she had tasted a Greek pastry many years before and how much she had enjoyed it. She also stated she couldn't remember the name of the pastry. I replied that it was probably baklava. She went on and on about how much she enjoyed baklava, but she had not been able to find it since. Sometimes you just have to believe in luck. We had a gentleman in our office who was Greek and who baked excellent baklava. I asked him to bake a batch, which I sent by airfreight to the assistant's boss. I enclosed a little note to the boss saying I would appreciate it if he would give the baklava to his assistant. Was I trying to gain something by sending the gift to the boss instead of the assistant? You bet! I truly like to do nice things for people, but sometimes I want others to know what I have done. It's called marketing yourself.

The bottom line; we saw a tiny opportunity and we acted on it. We eventually landed our first trial order after several attempts to bring new product ideas to the company. But, in the end we failed. Why, because our local salesperson relied on me to bring all of the new product ideas and to form the relationships with individuals at the company. The sales person who doesn't take on the responsibility to personally develop the business relationship will never live up to his/her sales potential. You cannot count on someone else to always make good things happen for you and your clients.

The key to forming lasting relationships is to begin working on the relationship the very first visit and to never stop. Avoid treating customers, prospects, or business associates as fair weather friends. Remember, you start forming the relationship in the first seven seconds and it is up to you whether or not the relationship continues.

Selling is fundamentally an interaction between people. The best sales people are "people persons." That is, they genuinely like and respect other people and enjoy encounters with different individuals presented by the selling process. Sales people often tell me that it takes too much work to form relationships. Yes, it takes extra effort, time and money to build solid relationships with several members of an organization, some of whom may seem insignificant. But if an account is valuable, sales professionals know they must extend their relationship building beyond the primary contact or the buyer. The very best actually enjoy doing it.

A gentleman came to my office for a meeting, and we had a great visit. When he left, my assistant came in to share several things with me. As she was leaving I said, "I'm really going to like doing business with that guy." She looked back over her shoulder at me and said, "If you like that kind." I asked her what she meant by the comment and she told me how the visitor had treated her with indifference, boarding on being down right rude. After hearing about such Jekyll and Hyde behavior, do you think that person made a sale with me? No Sir!

Cultivate Good Communication Skills

Forming lasting business relationships requires a person to display three things: integrity, talent and good communication skills. All three of these characteristics are important, but good communication skills are vital. Studies show seven of 10 business people who lose their jobs do so because of poor communication skills. Alert! You can be the nicest person in the world, but if you do not know how to communicate with others about your company and its offerings, you'll never be successful at selling. There are plenty of books and tapes on the market to help you improve your speaking and writing skills. Courses are offered at your local college. If you have a weakness in this area, brush up immediately.

Be Interesting, Knowledgeable And Humorous

The best sales people usually are fun. They also are interesting and knowledgeable. What's more, people enjoy their company and like to be around them. To be very successful at selling, you must be interesting, knowledgeable and fun, too.

Read the daily newspaper and a broad selection of magazines. This will give you the ability to discuss non-business matters such as sports, current affairs and other topics that happen to come up in a conversation with clients and customers. Try to find something in common with the customer, so the customer will find it easier to relate to you. Once you find a common ground, it's easier to develop a relationship.

To me, work is fun! That's because I try to have fun even in the most dismal situations. For example, boarding an airplane can be tedious, especially when everything stops because passengers who are placing their baggage in the overhead bins back up traffic in the aisle. When this happens, I like to say to those around me, while looking out the window at the wing of the plane, "Wow, that is the biggest crack I have ever seen on an airplane wing." Not everyone appreciates the joke, but those who have a sense of humor usually burst out laughing, thus relieving the tension brought on by boarding.

Speaking of air travel, once I was sitting in the first class section on a short flight. Because the flight was less than an hour and a half long, our meal service consisted of a small sandwich - which was perfectly fine with me. Unfortunately, the gentleman in front of me was not satisfied and hit his overhead call button several times. When the flight attendant did not come immediately, he began to hit the call button again and again.

Eventually, the flight attendant came to ask how she could be of service. The gentleman commented very loudly, "This is a bad sandwich, this is a bad sandwich — you people ought to be ashamed of yourself for serving such a bad sandwich."

The flight attendant picked up his sandwich tray, shook her finger at the sandwich as if scolding it and said, "You are a bad sandwich; you are a bad sandwich." She put the sandwich tray back down and walked off with a big smile on her face. I believe this woman loved her job and she wasn't going to let anyone take the fun out of it! Having fun and loving what you do becomes evident to everyone around you and it can be a powerful selling advantage.

With regards to using humor in the selling process, I'm not talking about telling jokes. I am talking about cultivating a style of humor that can break down business and personal barriers. A recent survey of corporate personnel directors reported 84 percent of those polled felt employees that had a sense of humor do a better job than those without one. They felt a sense of humor is a characteristic that can be used to build quality relationships in the workplace. This makes sense. While customers are pragmatic about their purchasing decisions, when the time comes to award the contract they often overrule their logic and choose to buy from the person who brings them joy and relief from the stress of the job.

Since customers like to be around people who are fun to be with, I like to tell relevant funny stories to customers so they can laugh once or twice during my visit or telephone contact. To add to my repertoire, I read the humor sections in Reader Digest in hopes of seeing a funny story that I can tuck away in the back of my mind and use when the appropriate time arrives. I also purchase two to three humor books every year that give me ideas on how to use humor in selling.

Some people are naturally funny. They are quick to make a

humorous comment, a play on words or a witty remark. Being quick witted and able to make funny comments is a gift. The extraordinarily gifted, like actor Robin Williams, can make a fortune from their talents. Few, however, are naturally funny. That doesn't mean one cannot improve his use of humor as a communication tool. If necessary, read books that deal with humor and try to retain those stories you can use later with clients.

If humor is not your greatest asset, study it. Remember, using humor makes it more fun for others to be with you. Furthermore, you will be judged on the joy and value you bring prospective clients. That is, do you help them do their job better and do you brighten their day?

Another way to stay in contact with customers and prospects and also display your sense of humor is to send humorous post cards. Post cards with a humorous message can be a potent weapon in your arsenal. Consider a customized post card with a special message that reflects your personality and has a sketch or photo of you printed on the card.

When I read a humorous article in the newspaper that's appropriate for customers or associates, I send it just for their enjoyment. Recently, there was an article in a Phoenix newspaper about a town in Arizona called Nothing. Only five people lived in the town. In the article the writer related the trials and tribulations the town's folk endured with rattlesnakes and occasional big city visitors. The article played up the lack of civic pride they felt living in a town called Nothing. The article was so funny; I took it to a printer and made 150 copies. I mailed one to each of my clients and business associates. The response I received from the mailing was eventually more than 30 percent. The point is, the mailing initiated a contact from the recipient and kept our relationship current. Selling is easier when you establish a relationship that appears to be more than just a business one.

Evaluate The Relationship

How many gifts do you get from customers in comparison to those you give? When your important customers have a Christmas party, retirement party or a company outing, are you one of the vendor/sales representatives invited to the event? Most businesses have favorite vendors and sales representatives who are considered extensions of the sales and management team. If your customers do not occasionally pay for your business meals or entertainment, you might want to examine why. If you have to "buy" the business by always paying for the meals and entertainment, I believe something might be wrong with the business relationship.

Early in my sales career, I had a customer in which sales grew from nothing to about $250,000 in sales annually. The purchasing manager and the vice president of sales and marketing continuously asked me to bring my golf clubs on my next visit. I heard them tell me they would like to play golf together. To be honest with you, I thought one of the reasons they asked me to bring my clubs was so I could pay for their golf game.

I didn't play golf with these customers for quite awhile. That's because the logical side of my brain told me taking time to have fun wasn't compatible with my work ethic. My territory covered all of Georgia and Florida, and I convinced myself playing golf with customers was wasting valuable sales and prospecting time. At that point, I did not understand how important relationships are to sales success. I did a pretty good job initiating relationships, but I wasn't as good as I should have been at nurturing them.

Several months later, I brought my golf clubs telling the client in advance I would be doing so. To my surprise, we went to their country club. They paid for not only the golf, but for the meal and all the beverages! I had misread their motives completely. This customer wanted to show appreciation for some hard work and value added services I had provided. The pay back for both of us was the opportunity to share on the golf course ideas and needs with one another from which both parties could benefit. From that moment on, I revised my business activities to pay attention to what my customers really wanted. If they wanted to play golf, and their sales volume or potential volume warranted it, I played golf!

Look For Chances To Do Something Special

While serving as vice president for sales and marketing at a food manufacturing concern, I attended a convention in Hawaii. There I had the opportunity to meet a prospect my firm had been calling on for a long time without success. During the convention, the prospect and I had the opportunity to spend some quality time together. He asked me to sit with him at the convention dinner that night. Everything was shaping up for a great relationship until another gentleman, who liked to hear the continuous sound of his own voice, sat at our table and consumed the entire conversation.

My prospect mentioned to the other gentleman that his 15-year old son collected unusual Coca-Cola cans. If you have ever known anyone that collected beer cans or soda cans as a hobby, you will appreciate the unbelievable fervor with which they go about their hobby. Upon hearing about the prospect's son, I immediately made a note about his hobby The next day, I called our corporate office and asked an associate to get in contact with the national and international sales force requesting them to send me unusual Coke cans as quickly as possible. I then called our representative in Boston and asked her to make an appointment with the prospect so that I could hand deliver the cans.

When I went to see the client, the visit was proceeding with cold courtesy. I was immediately aware the prospect still had a stronger relationship with our competitor. You see, we had as yet done nothing special to bring extra value to anyone or any department at that organization. Near the end of the visit, the client asked me what was in the boxes. I stated, "Coca-Cola cans for your son." His eyes got big and he jumped out of his chair and began cutting open the four boxes of cans. He wanted to know how I knew about his son's hobby and I replied that I had heard him tell a gentleman at the convention dinner in Hawaii.

He called in the other decision-makers, an agreement was reached and I walked out of the meeting with a trial order. That was in mid-December. Right after the beginning of the New Year, I got a letter from our new customer, which stated,

> *Dear Bill, I want you to know how happy we are with our new relationship. I have enclosed another order and... P.S. I did want to tell you what I did with the Coca-Cola cans you brought for my son. I put two of the little six-ounce cans from Europe in his Christmas stocking with a note telling him there were four more boxes of Coke cans underneath the Christmas tree. Bill, he loved that gift more than the new motorcycle I gave him.*

Wow, I was a real hero! Smart people in sales keep their eyes and ears open to hear about the little things they can do that can make a big difference in establishing or nurturing a long-term business relationship.

Recognize Milestones

Client's birthdays are important to recognize. Each year I send a telegram to my parents congratulating them on such a great event — my birthday! Just kidding. Sending a birthday card to the buyer and members of the purchasing or accounting departments' support staff cultivates loyalty and sends a signal that you appreciate them as people and not simply as customers who generate or process orders and payments.

Several years ago, the local sales rep and I were making a call on a purchasing agent at a Fortune 500 company. The agent had a picture of her five-year-old daughter in her ballerina costume on her desk. During the conversation, I found out two things. First, the daughter had outgrown her ballerina slippers and would have to wait about six months before she could get a new pair. The daughter could not continue her ballet lessons, because she did not have slippers that fit. Moreover, the mother, a single parent and part-time student, could not afford to continue the lessons.

Later in the conversation, I also found out that the mother had a birthday the next week. After we checked out the gift policy at that particular corporation, the sales rep called back to schedule a birthday luncheon for the next day. At the luncheon, the local sales representative gave her an envelope, which included a gift certificate for a pair of ballet slippers. The mother was ecstatic. The way I look at it, we were helping people achieve their goals with our gift and we were not trying to buy business. Did we hope that we were looked at in a more favorable light? Of course we did. Apparently, many people before us had also seen the photo with the ballet slippers. If they had asked the right questions, they also would have known the shoes no longer fit. We got the order.

Career promotions of client's employees also offer another great opportunity to begin or strengthen a relationship. If you've been promoted, you know the feeling of accomplishment and pride. I'm sure you will agree that promotions are very important events in the career lives of individuals. Those promoted usually are deserving of the recognition and advancement, so smart sales persons send a congratulatory note. Sounds easy enough!

Give Unusual Gifts

I like to capitalize on my business gift giving by carefully selecting unusual items. Because I live in Arizona, I want clients to remember where I'm from, as a method of distinguishing me from my competitors. For example, I often bring along a small gift package containing three jars of salsa manufactured by the daughters of the distinguished former United States Senator, Barry Goldwater. I also tell my clients or prospects the salsa company is a business neighbor. The gift has impact because the name Goldwater is widely recognized.

Once I sent a clear glass bowl that contained colored sand and cactus plants to a female client in Scottsdale, Arizona. Seven years elapsed before I had the opportunity to visit her again. The first thing I saw in her office was the gift that I had given to her years ago. She said, as she pointed to the cactus, "I have never forgotten you."

Another memorable gift I enjoy giving is a subscription to Arizona Highways magazine. Every month when a new issue arrives, my customers are reminded of me. Subscriptions to selected publications are fairly inexpensive and a great way to stay in touch on a regular basis.

To develop relationships with customers that have an ethnic background that is different from yours, you might want to send them printed articles you come across about their homeland. Another idea is to learn how to speak a few phrases or write a few lines in their native language.

My first sales territory was the states of Georgia and Florida. I was excited about doing business in Miami, which at the time had a population of approximately one million people. My home office, however, frankly told me to write off Miami. They said, "It is owned by the Cubans and they basically do business only with each other." I almost believed them. Instead of taking their advice, I found a Latin American college student who would call and make appointments with and write letters to Cuban prospects in Miami. Sure, the dialects were a little different, but the prospects could see that I was going the extra mile to try and do business with them. By being adaptable, my sales in the Cuban business sector increased significantly.

Show Appreciation

I recently sent a thank you note to an attorney for his help with an account. In the hand written thank you note, I enclosed a gift certificate from a certified massage therapist who would come to his office for a one-hour stress reduction massage. He called to say that he had never been offered such a unique gift of appreciation. Regardless of whether or not you send a gift, always send a handwritten thank you note to someone who has given you an order, made a referral, helped you get an appointment or provided valuable assistance. So little appreciation is shown in the business world that your tiny gesture will have enormous impact on the recipient.

Nurture Valued Relationships

To build and strengthen relationships, which are the key to business success, consider the following:

Always do what you promised – Nothing will kill a relationship quicker than someone who breaks promises. When a soldier falls asleep when he is on guard duty, would you trust him again to keep your camp safe? Lack of faith in someone is hard to overcome. Remember the last time someone let you down and how you felt about it. Don't let down your customers or prospects. Always write down whatever it is you promised to do, so you can follow-up later. If you can't keep your promises, call or write the individual to explain why.

Share your goals – Let the client know why you want to sell to them. Do not be afraid to share your desire to do the best you can at selling and your eagerness to do your best for the customer. When both parties know each other's goals, both can benefit from a relationship that meets the needs of each party.

Ask for feedback – True sales success is not just landing the account, it's keeping it forever. A professional relationship is one in which the customer is comfortable telling the vendor how they can improve. Customers want good people to be successful.

Be dependable – Customers and vendors that form strong partnerships perform for each other over the long haul. If you are involved in a sales contest, for example, and you need a little help to put you over the top, you can feel comfortable asking customers for help, just as they call on you for special help from time to time.

Three Key Assets

Three things make outstanding sales organizations. The first is the ability to use consultative selling techniques. The second is excellent general business skills. The third is the ability to form great relationships. Of the three, the ability to form lasting relationships is the most important. After all, it's easier to sell more to existing customers than to constantly prospect for new ones.

In addition, establishing great relationships with customers provides human rewards money alone can never give. One of the best benefits of selling is meeting and knowing interesting and wonderful people individuals who can truly enrich your life.

CHAPTER EIGHT

One Chance Selling

The long-term, consultative selling approach is not realistic or appropriate for many selling situations. Sometimes it is necessary to interest, excite, engage and sell the prospect in one brief encounter. Immediate selling situations occur in retail establishments, at trade shows and when making sales calls to a potential customer's home or office.

Each time you open your doors, exhibit at a trade show or make a sales call, it costs time and money. Therefore, successful entrepreneurs and business executives must attempt to get the maximum return for the investment. That means the selling effort must be productive.

Whether you sell crafts or computers, developing an effective sales presentation is fundamental to success. Sales experts maintain that a sales person must grab the attention of a shopper in 3.5 seconds. So, a well-conceived plan of attack is absolutely essential. Displays and sales presentation materials should be designed to attract shoppers and prospects. But, even with exceptional displays, sales will not occur if you are unable to communicate product information that is informative, professional and persuasive once the customer enters the store or the show booth.

All business revolves around selling. Money is made only when something is sold. Therefore, business owners and the sales staff must become comfortable with the selling process in order to succeed. Unfortunately, many merchants love to surround themselves with products they enjoy, but hate to sell them. Many manufacturers love to make their products, but have no idea about what to do at a trade show in order to obtain orders.

Much of the dislike for selling is derived from the notion that good sales people must be aggressive and pushy. With some preparation and practice, anyone can improve their selling skills and become comfortable making sales presentations without changing character or resorting to high-pressure selling tactics.

A Professional Attitude

Successful sales people must convey a friendly and helpful attitude. To make money selling products or services, the sales staff must enjoy dealing with people. Being pleasant to the customer is elementary, yet it is surprising how many people send out negative signals telegraphing their dislike for dealing with people.

Immediate selling situations also call for sales people to be well groomed and dressed appropriately, and to have a friendly demeanor to establish instant rapport with prospects, shoppers and buyers.

To maintain a professional attitude, the selling staff also should be prepared to respond to unhappy customers occasionally. Decide in advance how you will handle returns or how you will deal with unpleasant and demanding customers. Although unpleasant incidents are rare, if anticipated and discussed, the staff will know what to do or say when they occur. Always be prepared to handle these situations calmly and diplomatically.

Happy customers can be the source of substantial referral business. So, give some thought to your return policy and how you will deal with an unsatisfied customer. Studies show that unhappy customers will tell twice as many friends negative things about a business as happy customers tell positive things. It's human nature for people to complain more than to compliment. Since complaints can kill sales quickly, plan your responses carefully.

When involved in an immediate selling situation, remember to be friendly, but not too aggressive; informative, but not pushy; enthusiastic, but not overbearing. Experience will help you and your staff find the best selling personality.

Using Body Language To Your Advantage

Studies show that men and women send out certain strong messages just by the way they sit, stand or posture themselves. Standing with your arms crossed, for example, sends out a message to "keep your distance, don't come too close." Sales people can appear more approachable by keeping their arms at their sides or behind their back.

Making eye contact with potential customers projects warmth and friendliness. Try to catch the eye of all potential customers that come in the store or near the trade show booth. Then, greet them with a smile and a simple, "Hello" or "How are you doing today?" One study showed that by simply changing the greeting from "May I help you?" to "Have you been in our store before?" can increase sales 17 percent. Why? Because everyone says, "May I help you?" and most without an ounce of sincerity.

Avoid reading or occupying yourself with anything that does not pertain directly to presenting your products and selling. If you look too busy and don't acknowledge the customer's presence immediately, it is unlikely shoppers will approach you with questions. You will lose a chance to engage the prospect in conversation and qualify the person as a potential buyer.

On the other hand, do not look too idle, either. Busy yourself by straightening the stock, arranging the display or adding up receipts. Don't stand by the door or in the aisle looking as if you are ready to pounce on the first person that shows the slightest interest.

Today's buyers are on guard, and most resent the overly aggressive sales person. Successful selling begins when the sales person is able to tell the response and comfort level of the prospect by observing the shopper's body language.

Here is a simple technique you can use when the customer becomes uncomfortable as you approach the close of a sale. Take several steps backward or move away from the customer and busy yourself with something for a moment. Straighten a display or put something into the wastebasket. Watch the reactions of the customer and listen to the tone of voice. You will be amazed at how effective this gesture is for putting customers at ease and for letting them feel they are in control of the purchasing decision.

The study of body language has been the subject of many books and articles. Make some observations, read about the subject and incorporate what you learn in your selling methods. You will find applying this knowledge can make a difference in your sales effectiveness.

Your Sales Presentation

Think of immediate selling as the art of persuasive conversation. Learning what to say, as well as how and when to say it, is the key to increasing your sales and profits. Effective selling is really very simple. Susan Ratliff, an expert in exhibit marketing and merchandising, has a three-step approach. Just remember her three E's for successful selling: ENGAGE,

EXCITE, ENCOURAGE. You're probably thinking, "Sure, that sounds easy, but what exactly do I say?"

To start with, you cannot sit behind your counter or in the corner of the booth patiently waiting for customers to come over and ask you to ring up the sale or write the order. Some people actually believe their products will sell themselves. That's occasionally true, but research shows that initiating and following through with the proper selling process will generate many more sales.

Again, preparation is essential. To be comfortable with and capable at selling, you must be prepared. A sales presentation given by an accomplished sales person generally follows a pattern. First, the sales person approaches the prospect casually and starts a conversation with small talk. Then, the sales person proceeds to gain the potential customer's confidence while informing them of the product's assets in an unassuming manner. Through a series of questions and answers, the sales person qualifies the prospect. Finally, the sales person directs the customer to buy.

The sales presentation can be memorized and should vary from prospect to prospect only slightly. The best selling presentations are those that influence customers to buy, yet leave them pleased and satisfied that the decision to buy was their own.

For instant selling situations, develop an effective presentation by writing down what you wish to say to each potential customer. Next, memorize the presentation word for word. Practice with your family and friends until you feel confident and comfortable with what you are saying. Lack of attention to the basics often is the reason many fail to succeed in sales. Stick to the presentation and use it consistently with all prospects.

A good sales person must be attentive to the customer. This doesn't mean pouncing on everyone that comes within two feet of your products. It means keeping your eyes on their eyes. You are looking for the person who hesitates in front of a display, stares at a product from across the aisle, approaches with curiosity or stops to pick up an item. These cues indicate the customer wants to know more about the products.

When you notice these behaviors, it's time to make the critical first move to ENGAGE the prospect in a conversation and qualify the person as a potential buyer. Never start the conversation by saying, "May I help you?" The automatic response usually is, "No thanks, just looking."

Instead, use what Susan Ratliff calls "SHOPPER STOPPERS." Shopper stoppers are special questions or statements that compel the customer to stay and talk with you. First, make eye contact, then say something like, "Hi, have you been in our store (visited our booth) before?" Or, "Good morning, my name is Jane, please make yourself at home and just call out 'Jane' when I can serve you."

When politely responded to, you might say, "These T-shirts are 100 percent cotton and preshrunk," to the person standing by the T-shirt counter.

Or, "These handbags were hand-tooled in Italy. I selected them on my buying trip there last month. They are so unusual. What color are you looking for?"

Or, "How old is the child you have in mind for this toy? We carry toys suitable for children one through four in this section."

Or, "Mr. Jones, would you prefer to have me escort you around the car lot to show you the different models or would you prefer to browse alone?"

Or, "This new laptop computer model features a wireless Internet connection; let me show you how great this works."

These are just a few examples of opening lines that attempt to ENGAGE customers and either make them stop and talk more, which indicates that a sale is possible, or force them to quickly answer and move on, which means they weren't interested and you saved yourself a lot of time.

Always remember the purpose of your effort is to make sales. Be sure you have interested, qualified customers before you take up your time and their time giving a sales presentation. Many people will be just browsing. If you spend time repeating the presentation to everyone, without thought to the prospect's financial ability to buy, timing, authority to purchase or desire for the products, you will wear yourself out and generate very few sales. Every person pursued should be a qualified buyer. With a little experience, potential customers can be spotted easily.

After the prospect has been qualified and shows continued interest, a successful salesperson moves on to step two, EXCITE! When appropriate, put the product in the customer's hands. Let them feel it, try it on or see how it works. Confirm that you have the right size, the right color, and you can ship anywhere, if that's what it takes to make the sale. Offer information of interest that will create desire for your product. If you are selling something made by hand, tell the prospect how difficult it is to make, discuss the rarity of the materials used or the uniqueness of the design.

Product Knowledge Is Essential

If you are an exclusive manufacturer or dealer of a product line or the buyer who travels to Hong Kong and personally selects each item, be sure to inform the shopper. Enthusiasm sells, but product knowledge sells more. So, take pride in your work and learn as much as possible about the products you are selling.

If you are selling a business product or personal service, you should demonstrate the benefits of the offerings. Show prospects what the service will do for them. Explain the extent of the warranty and tell why the product is better than others on the market. Indicate when delivery is possible; talk about quality and demonstrate performance.

When you feel prospects are convinced of what they need and want and what you offer, proceed to step three. ENCOURAGE them to buy it, now. A simple, closing statement like, "May I wrap that up for you?" or "Let me show you our best payment schedule," will either result in the sale or bring up an objection. When potential customers present objections, they are saying, "sell me more!" The entire persuasive conversation or sales presentation takes only a matter of minutes.

Why People Buy

There are two reasons why shoppers and buyers make purchases. First, they are attracted to the product or service. The second reason, and many times the real reason the sale is made, is because the customer likes the sales person. Sales people who are always friendly, helpful and informative can influence how customers feel about their products. People enjoy buying from sales people who are excited about what they sell and who enjoy their work. Again, enthusiasm often can compensate for a lack of sales expertise.

In addition, shoppers often will buy a product simply because they discovered something in common with the sales person. To increase sales, always try to find a common bond with prospects. During a sales presentation you may discover you're both from the same hometown, your kids go to the same school, or you both have a Labrador Retriever. Believe it or not, these personal links often can be the reason a customer will buy from you and not from your competitor. While trying to establish a link, never be too pushy or too talkative, and never get upset if you don't make the sale.

Overcoming Objections

Even if you are friendly and informative and able to give a great sales pitch, not every potential customer will be an easy sell. A person may hesitate to buy because an item is too expensive, too small, too large, not the right color, or a myriad of other reasons. These objections usually don't surface directly. Probe for objections throughout your conversation and listen for clues that will uncover the reasons shoppers are hesitating. When someone gives you an objection, remember they really are telling you "sell me more."

When you think you know what is preventing the prospect from making the purchase, confront him with it. If you think the problem is price, you might say, "I have several payment schedules available with no interest for six months. Which of these plans sound good to you?" The customer, at this point, might reveal the true problem. "I have to consult my partners first before I make this purchase." If you think the problem is color or size and you can provide other choices not displayed, you might say, "I can get these dresses in blue or yellow, too. Were you looking for a different color?" The buyer, at this point, might reveal the true problem, like "Our store has so many dresses, we really need to stock more shorts and pants."

Learning to overcome objections is a very important part of your sales presentation. After developing your sales pitch, make a list of every excuse a customer might use for not purchasing your merchandise. Next, write down what you will say as a rebuttal to each objection. Memorize your rebuttals and be prepared to use them when the customer presents an objection.

It often takes as many as six attempts to close a sale before the sale is made. The reason many people fail at sales is not because they can't sell, it's because they quit too soon. Wait until the customer says "no" five times. Then, try again. Most sales are made after the fifth "no."

Selling is an art. The more you and your sales staff learn about selling, the more you can earn for your business. Don't underestimate the need to acquire knowledge and expertise in selling. Read as many books on the subject as you can. Attend workshops and seminars to improve selling skills. Observe and imitate other individuals who have excellent sales skills. The extra effort will pay off and help your business or career grow and prosper.

Add-On Selling

The next time you eat at a fast food restaurant listen carefully to what the cashier says after you place an order. You probably will be asked if you would like an order of fries or a soft drink to go with your meal. This seemingly simple gesture is a calculated sales technique. It's one of the reasons why McDonald's is the leader in the fast food trade. All competitors now follow suit, but McDonald's pioneered the technique of the add-on sale. The goal of add-on selling is to get every customer to buy more than they originally intended.

By simply suggesting the customer might like a pair of slacks to go with the skirt and jacket or a computer dust jacket for the new laptop computer, a sales person may be able to increase the dollar amount of the sale substantially. Combine, match, pair or accessorize as many products as you can. You will be surprised how this will increase the dollar amount of each sale. Since you already have an interested customer, who is ready to make one purchase, it is easier to sell more to that customer than to start over with another one.

Be Respectful

If you are calling on offices and come across a "No Solicitors" sign, do not ignore it. If someone ignores the sign in our office, we do not give the individual any consideration whatsoever. If the sales person does not respect our wishes, why should be care about him/her? Visitors are welcome to drop off fliers, however. We usually read them because they announce special offers or new businesses in the immediate area. Most businesses with "No Solicitors" signs will not object to distribution of information. It's also acceptable to enter an office to request a business card in order to call for an appointment later. Never, never attempt to make a drop-in sales presentation at an establishment that tells you with a "No Solicitors" sign that you are not welcome.

You've Got To Be Good

Sometimes the immediate sale and the instant close are more difficult to accomplish than sales through long-term relationship selling, even when you have an interested buyer. If you are not good in the very first minute of the encounter, you will probably not make the sale unless the buyer is desperate to have what you offer. Therefore, like most things, you've got to be good to be successful at immediate selling. Being good takes practice, practice, and more practice.

CHAPTER NINE

Top Gun Salesperson

I speak and consult in a wide range of industries and I find it hard to find 1 or 2% of the sales personnel that would be classified as great.

Shocking? It should not be because most corporations hire sales personnel that have never been trained, educated and held accountable for greatness. Following their hiring, almost all of them are again not provided with training and education. And then one of them is later named Vice President of Sales – without any skills training and education to be a great Vice President of Sales. The cycle goes on and on resulting in less sales and reduced margins than could be achieved.

Those individuals wanting and needing to be in the top 2% take charge of their own destiny. What do they do? Read on.

Work Hard On Themselves

They work harder on themselves than they do for their employer. Who wins with this philosophy? Everyone wins, the individual, the clients, and the employer.

Most industry representatives do not read every trade magazine in their industry. Read. Be an expert. I read over 400 trade magazines monthly. Yep, that's 400+. Would you hire a speaker or consultant who had stopped reading and learning? No! And do clients want to deal with a sales person who has gone stale? No. And don't just read magazines in your industry. Read magazines from other industries to help you get out of your box. They are usually free. If you don't read, you don't grow.

Trustworthy

Over 80% of all clients make their vendor selection because they like, trust and respect the sales person. Ask yourself what you are doing to get prospective clients to like, trust and respect you. You have to earn a great reputation as a leader or else you will be stuck in the role of selling something, to somebody, at a price. That's not a profession, but a boring job. Think hard about this paragraph.

Generous

Are you a giver? Do you give more of yourself to your clients and employer than anyone else does? The top 2% do. If you receive more gifts from clients than you give out, you're in the top 2%. If you pay for golf every time, you're not. You have to give a lot to get a lot. Give your best stuff to everyone.

If you are not in the habit of giving, the next time you exit a tollbooth, pay for the person behind you. And don't let them catch up to you to see who you are. It drives them nuts.

Helpful to Client

Think of and for clients at all times. Do you cut articles out and mail them to clients. Don't just read for your personal benefit. Read with the eyes of a "servancy business person". If you see an article that would be interesting and beneficial for a client, send it to them so they will find you to be – interesting and beneficial.

Value-Added

Be a value-added sales professional. Figure out how you will provide unheard of services that no one else offers. If you don't, you better hope that I do not provide field training for your competitor – and close 90% of you "former" clients.

Creative

Be more creative than ever before. Always think and act on this question: "what am I going to do to make this the best sales visit they have ever seen"? And be creative before and after the visit. Creativity (emotion) beats logic (technical) almost every time in sales. Win them over emotionally first followed by the details later.

Pro Change

Winners understand they can't be status quo. They know that they will never arrive. Even if you become the best in the world, you can't remain the best if you start feeling and acting as if "I have arrived." No Matter how good you are today, you can be 25% better in 90 days. And over 90% of all the sales representatives I have worked with could become 50% better – yes, 50% better. Grow or perish.

Certified

Those that are serious about their profession become certified. Sales people are like consultants in that only 1 in about 25,000 become certified. I'm certified in both of my professions, a CMC and CPS after my name means that I have earned them – and I earn more. My two big needs are money and oxygen; and designations bring me more of one of them. Earn yours.

Businessperson

Don't be a sales person – be a fantastic businessperson. Fridays are a great day to be such a person. I suggest you forget about making sales calls on most Friday afternoons. How many visits can you make between 1:00 and 5:00? 1? 2? Work at your desk instead. Mail 15 postcards, make 15 phone calls and get organized. Once a month, invest an all-day at your desk and mail 25 postcards, make 25 phone calls and act on every item in this article. Beats 3 or 4 prospect and service visits almost every time.

Leader

Be a leader in your association. Be a good speaker, serve on a committee or/and run for an office. The message is: don't do what 98% do which is to just show up at the convention or trade shows. Most trade show booths look just like they did the year before. Most advertisements look like they did the year before. Prepare now for you to be different at next years show. You will gain respect.

Look Professional

Look, act and be the part. Do you remember that Kennedy beat Nixon in the first televised debate? Kennedy looked the part and spoke with vigor or "vigah" as he pronounced it. He had it all that night: dark suit, tanned appearance and enthusiasm. Nixon sweated and looked pale in his gray suit. Historians state that the election was won that night. Kennedy looked and acted the part to get the part he wanted. And, by the way, Nixon "won" according to the radio listeners due to his content. Get a consultant to help you with your appearance, style and actions. Then get an engineer to help you with the technical side. Not the technical stuff first.

Planning

Prepare and stick to a plan. 98% of salespeople operate without a solid plan because as they say "I don't have time to plan." Start with a 12-month plan and work it backward into quarters, to the month, to the week and then by the day.

Who are your next 10 clients going to be? When will they come on board? Which products will they buy? And how much will they buy? And how am I going to make it happen? Don't know? Then you are drifting. I'm not talking about an unrealistic marketing plan. I'm talking about a sales action plan. And review it weekly to <u>beat</u> deadline dates.

Focus

Develop a Target Account Program. Start by identifying the 3, 5 or 10 accounts that merit an all-out effort by you and your associates. Then list every action you will take with deadline dates. Do more for them than anyone else has done before. Many sales people start to settle in after they land an account. Catch those settled-in sales people flat-footed.

The clients I work with land 7 to 10 of every 10 targeted clients due to a focused effort. And don't forget objectives like what kind of "un-heard of personal value will I deliver to them?" Can't think of 1 or 2? You're not thinking.

Ideas

Keep a voice recorder on your front seat to capture ideas that pop out of your brain when you least expect it. Use it to dictate letters while driving. "Not any big deal" you might be thinking, Well, it is. One, you don't want to forget the ideas. Secondly, why dictate letters in your office when it could have been done in driving time? Pick up just 5 minutes a day and you will gain 20 ½ hours annually.

Time Management

Manage your time like it is your major currency – because it is. Major time should be invested into major things such as Target Accounts. Minor time should be spent on minor things such as minor accounts. Don't spend the same amount of time with someone who can buy $50,000 as you do with a $500,000 client. Harness your time so you have more time to make more money. I wrote this article on the weekend – not between 8:00 AM – 5:00 PM on a weekday. 8:00 – 5:00 on weekdays is client time.

Role Model

Choose your role model carefully. Pick someone who is in the top 1-2%. It may even be a competitor. Ask, "who am I currently hanging around and what are they doing to me"? If you make $50,000 and truly want to make $150,000, do you hang around someone earning $50,000 or someone earning $150,000? New entries to the speaking and consulting professions call and write constantly asking for my help as their role model. They hardly ever offer to help me in return. And if I finally ask for their help, I get "I'm too stressed out" or "I'm too busy right now." These individuals will never make it to the top. They think WIIFM (what's in it for me) and not "how can I try to repay you"? They are takers that don't believe in the "give to get" philosophy I shared earlier. One person I have given hundreds of hours told me today "I will do it tomorrow". He asked for my help weekly. The message is to mimic your role model. Try to, at least, help them as much as they help you.

Training And Education

Encourage your corporation to invest in training and 1 on 1 education. They invest in equipment and more equipment, but few are progressive enough to invest an adequate amount into training and education. If your employer is too short-sighted to understand, invest into 1 on 1 training for yourself. It's not a cost. It's an investment. It will come back to you in big-time dollars.

Contemplation

Take a little quiet time once in a while. While serving as Vice President of Sales and Marketing, I used to send the entire sales force off, twice a year, to a park, hotel room or wherever just to think. No phones. They took their annual plan, day planners, position descriptions, etc. They were to think, "What am I doing that I should not be doing?" and "what am I not doing that I should be doing"? The brain works much better when there is no stress and no noise interruptions. I spend 100 days a year providing 1-on-1 executive and sales coaching – and I conduct the sessions without interruptions. These sessions are better than classroom training any day. Why, because we focus just on the specific challenges for one specific person. Go alone or arrange for a 1-on-1 coaching session. Use your brain not the odometer or frequent flier miles.

Needs Analysis

Conduct a needs analysis with every prospect and every client. Always ask a question such as "how can I personally serve you better"? With a prospect that you have called on for a while, try "Sir, I have been calling on you for 17 months without success. I must be doing something wrong. Will you please tell me what it is"? Whatever the questions are, listen intently to every response, take great notes, and act. Great selling is listening – not talking.

Open To Change

Be open to change — really open because being in the top 2% will probably require radical adjustments. This is a fast – changing world. Be ahead of the curve or leave the profession. We change jobs, friends and spouses. Why not us?

All business is primarily people business. Who develops and produces the products? Sells it? Buys it? People. I make sales calls for my clients all over the world and I ask for the toughest ones – and we close 90% of them. And…I know little to almost nothing about the industries. I can get the technical information from my client's technical personnel. My job is to get my client's clients to **WANT** to buy from us – and **NEED** us. How? Just start with the above steps.

Just about anyone (some are not meant to be in this profession) can be in the top 2%. This applies to sales departments and sales representatives. Will it be tough? Of course it will. Are individual and corporate **greatness** worth the prices to pay?

It's a very easy answer for smart and progressive people.

CHAPTER TEN

Get CRAZEE

You must be CRAZEE if you want to sell and lead with gusto. After all, who wants to be thought of as boring? And yet, most sales people are boring. Most business telephone calls are boring. Even business letters are boring. Be anything but boring!

Be CRAZEE — a word I've coined to emphasize the traits that set leaders and sales people apart from the pack.

C Is For Creativity

You can write with one hand or hop on one leg, but you have to engage both sides of your brain to sell with gusto. Both sides? Yes, the left side is where the logical communications take place. Speaking and listening with only the left side, or logical side, of the brain makes Jack a dull boy. The right side is where creativity resides.

Almost one-half of all men and the majority of women use the right side of their brain (the creative side) more than the left side (logical) when it is time to make a decision. The trick is to use both sides of your brain when you're trying to sell an idea, product or service, and you will almost always send your message home. Sell with all logic or all creativity and the chances are high you will miss the mark. There is more on Creativity in the following chapter.

R Is For Regimen

A very small percentage of all sales people have a regimen to be proud of. This small percentage has identified the clients they want to obtain for the year. They have laid out a concrete plan to obtain between 70-90% of those identified. The plan may include up to 25 specific things they are going to do to take the business away from a competitor. And, they set deadline dates for all 25 specific actions. That's regimen.

A Is For Ambition

Most of the sales and management personnel I have known over the years worked hard to very hard. The problem is, however, many seem to settle into a routine and become stagnant. Doing the same not-so-productive activities time and time again.

Do you know someone who seems old at 40? How about old at 30? I see it often. They lacked fire and determination – they've settled in. They have stopped their self-improvement program.

If you're a manager, don't settle in. Your own ambition and fire will shine on your face and it will encourage others to exhibit the same behaviors. You set the tone – and others will follow.

Z Is For Zany

Being zany is similar to being creative, only more so. It is the ability to do unusual and even silly things by design, and win loyalty or more business because people enjoy working with people who are fun to be with.

Adding a touch of zaniness makes you more memorable than the average person. Remember, when you're average, you're just as close to the bottom as you are to the top. Whether you sell doors, chickens, trucks or aircraft engines, being "off the wall" occasionally beats any dull routine.

What is the one zany thing you did today? Yesterday? What three zany things did you do last week? What zany things are you going to do next week? Can't think of any? Then you are stuck!

EE Is For Emotional Equivalent

I consider EE much more important than IE (intellectual excellence). Emotional equivalent is your attitude about who you are, who you want to become, whom you seek to emulate, what you want to contribute in personal relationships, and what you see as life's challenges.

Some people are self-serving while others seek out ways to serve. Some take and some give. Some think of selling things for money while others just love what they do, knowing that the money will follow. EE can be taught and learned. It can be enhanced just as an IE can be.

I believe CRAZEE is an acronym for a well-balanced businessperson because CRAZEE works everywhere. Think not? Then just stack the deck with NON-CRAZEE individuals and here's what you get:

NON-C: "No, that will never work here."
NON-R "I don't have enough time to do that."
NON-A: "That's not my job."
NON-Z: "You think that's funny?"
NON-EE: "Everyone here is a jerk (except me)."

Crazy to write about CRAZEE? I don't think so.

CHAPTER ELEVEN

Top Gun Creativity

"Using only one side of the brain when selling means selling from the wrong side!" — William Blades

"Creativity is the sudden cessation of stupidity" — Edwin Land

There are two sides of the brain — left and right; left is the logical side and right is our creative side. This is nothing magical thus far. What is magic is the ability to inject a more than adequate dosage of the creative side of the brain when you are attempting to sell a product or service. The vast majority of people, with the exception of accountants, buy from the right side of the brain. That is, they will often buy emotionally (right side) and justify it logically (left side).

Some Examples

When Lexus arrived on the scene, I just had to have a new LS 400. It was an emotional decision that I was going to buy one! I sat in the cushy leather seats, turned on all of the toys like the memory seats and the CD player (which already had a rack of discs stored in the trunk!) and visualized how much I would love this car. I was an easy sell because I buy almost everything, except computers, by emotion.

The sales person almost blew it! He started talking about the pounds-per-square inch of air in the oversized tires. He was talking himself right past the sale. In other words, he was about to "buy it back." The amount of air in a tire was logical selling and he was missing the boat entirely. I have yet to learn how air travels from the air filter down to the tires anyway.

On the way home, I started to justify logically what I had purchased. Lexus has a 1-inch square telephone speaker on the steering wheel — what a neat toy! I used the telephone to call my wife. I told her that the car would hold its value, it had roadside service 24 hours-a-day, and blah-blah-blah. She knew what I was doing — justifying my emotional purchase. Logically, we may need a new car or a new outfit, but when we see that one item, we think "Wow, that's me." A logical purchase, but the exacting choice was made emotionally.

Why do most sales people sell from the left side of the brain when almost everyone buys from the right side? Because someone in the 1950's trained a salesperson that way, and the recipient of that training taught someone else the same way and the cycle continued. This pattern creates the need for unlearning the way we were taught to sell. Often a salesperson will call their boss and state that their customer felt the price was "too high." Hardly ever is it price. In most cases, the buyer just feels more comfortable with his/her current supplier. The potential buyer also is thinking "This person has not yet convinced me." Maybe that salesperson has been selling with too much of one side of his/her brain while the buyer has used the opposite side. No sale.

Intuition

A recent study points out that women are guided much more by right side thinking and intuition, than men. They also tend to utilize both sides of the brain than most males who are more logic driven. The following numbers represent the decision-making unit that men and women rely on most:

	Logic	Intuition
Men	71%	29%
Women	47%	53%

There are many observations we could draw from these numbers, but one that I picked up on is that, in all probability, 71% of male salespersons sell predominately with a logical bent. Most of them, I believe, could benefit from studying how female buyers think and then adjusting their style accordingly.

At the other end of the scale, one cannot approach a financial-type buyer (accountant) with creative selling. Almost always, they want and need your charts, graphs and numbers. They love that stuff. For them, utilize an 80/20 presentation (80% logic). However, if you were to give me charts and graphs, I will mentally take a hike during your presentation. With me, you would need to offer ideas that could benefit me. You would come into my office and just get on with it — fast paced with lots of energy. That is what gets my attention and moves me because you would have hit an emotional hot button.

Another Example

One of the best sales calls I have ever witnessed happened about 10 years ago. After being "put to sleep" continuously by left-brained salespeople who went on-and-on about their features and benefits (that really were neither), a lady came in to see me and pulled-off a spectacular sale.

Upon entering my office, I shook her hand and asked her to take a seat while I went to get us some coffee. She said, "If it is all right, I would rather stand." When I asked her "why," she replied, "Because I have done my homework on you and I was told to get in and get out quickly." I inquired as to who might have advised her on how to conduct her visit. She then furnished the names of two people who knew my style well. She had indeed done her homework because I like salespeople to be brief, be bright and be gone. She was all three. She was selling advertising for a trade magazine and on her first visit to me (after trying for two years), she landed a nice chunk of our ad budget. I called her sales manager and told him about how she had "done her homework," laid her presentation out with logic, hit me with the "wow" part, and proceeded to hit a home-run. I asked that he congratulate her in front of her peers at their next sales meeting. Conclusion: she modified her style to match my style — smart.

Habits

As humans, we tend to do things by habit. In the sales world this means we sell today almost the same way we did 5 and 10 years ago. Not good. Many sales reps get in the car, make a call, get in the car, make another call etc., all without much preplanning as to how they are going to "blow their client's socks off with consultative and relationship selling. I suggest to salespeople that planning must be made with the thought in mind of "How am I going to be worthy of their respect?" or "What can I offer this client that no one else has ever offered?" Above all do not be boring! If you prefer to be boring, move to Oklahoma and get in the oil drilling business. There, boring is good.

If you drive to your office on a regular basis, you probably take the same route. A habit. Often you will be thinking about a lot of things as you maneuver your car through the city in the same way you do every day. The driving habit has been ingrained in your mind that you can think of many things while driving and your brain will subconsciously place your car in the parking lot... right? The key is to break habits and work harder on growing yourself. That is, work harder on yourself than you do for your employer. Your employer, however, will benefit from this goal. So will your clients. Remember, it is never the hours you put in or the number of miles that you place on the odometer. The bottom line is how effective you are.

Your brain is the one thing to be utilized to its maximum -

not your car or mouth. Keep your brain in idle motion and just listen to what is being said. Digest it and think later. Study people, study clients and hang around people that are wiser and more successful than you are. Ask the more successful ones how you can be more creative in approaching and solving clients' concerns and challenges.

I speak and consult internationally for sales groups. One thing I have concluded is that almost everyone, in every part of the world, does things by habit. They have just one selling style for everyone they sell to. This does not work. Just as there are no two fingerprints alike, there are no two clients just alike. Try to sell me like you do Mr. Bean Counter (customer prevention department), and you will probably fail. I tackle several retainer projects each year helping companies get out of second gear by offering ideas that will re-energize each individual's selling efforts. After every quarterly seminar, the top sales executive and I select 12 skills that we will hold everyone accountable for implementing. We might also add one or two more for "Bud" and one or two more for "Jane" based on their individual strengths and weaknesses. This means that everyone is held accountable for 48 new skills by yearend! How many sales representatives do you know that have placed just six new skills into practice last year? Hardly anyone. What do you think happens to the sales volume when the entire group is implementing 12 new skills every three months?

The key is to monitor and inspect the desired changes. You just cannot expect your entire sales force to embrace 12 new ideas quickly. Some will, but some are slow to CHANGE. Their logical side will often state, "That's just not my style to do that," "I don't have time," or "This is good for everyone else." To get your group to change, an investment in training and implementation services will be necessary. If a person sells logically, then he/she will need assistance in adapting to right side selling.

Examples Of Right-Side Selling And Thinking

- Ask for an 8:03 appointment with a prospective client rather than an 8:00 appointment. It makes you different before you ever even arrive.

- When asked, "How are you?" never say, "fine" like almost everyone does.

- Stop focusing on "Let's do lunch," and focus on obtaining as many breakfast appointments as you can. Clients are under less stress at 7:00 a.m. than they would be at noon. You also get more quality client visits in each day (Of course you let your waiter know in advance of your client's name so that he/she greets you and your client by name as you enter the restaurant).

- Recommend a speaker or consultant to the client. Recommend a great one that will position you as a hero. Sure beats trying to sell something to somebody at a price.

- For gifts, deliver a bag of gourmet coffee with your private label, or a book that the author inscribed for your client and tape your card next to the inscription.

- Take the client for breakfast in a hot air balloon. One breakfast in a hot air balloon beats 12 lunches annually at Holiday Inn almost every time.

- Delta ran an ad in USA Today that stated for every box of a certain type of Maxfli balls you bought, you would receive a free coach or first class companion ticket. I photocopied the ad and sent them to as many targeted clients I could think of. It was an effort to provide benefit through right side marketing. Millions of salespersons saw the ad and maybe 100,000 or so acted on the ad for themselves.

They saw only the "left side" or logical benefit for themselves.

I recommended the idea of photocopying the ad to a sales force of 14 people. Only one man came up to me at break time and asked for a copy of the Delta ad. Only one person thought

"Wow, neat idea" and 13 must have thought "That's dumb" because they didn't ask for it. Who's dumb?

Utilize a consultant to:
- Join you on a client visit — very progressive.

- Develop an audiotape for a particular client... a question and answer scenario with an introduction, music and hard-hitting benefits.

- Provide a seminar for your clients.

- Visit with your clients in your trade show booth to answer their best questions and challenges.

If you need a suggestion as to who provides the above services, let me know and I can tell you of a consultant who resides in Scottsdale, Arizona, who performs them really well. Hey, I'm a sales guy!

Examples Of Left-Side Selling And Thinking

- Find out everything you can about the client's needs and act on it. Remember that many of their needs have nothing to do with your offerings. Still act!

- Always go in to share information they may be interested in, and always ask questions so that you can learn something.

- Figure out how you will set yourself apart from the pack. Be an expert at something.

- Time is the currency of this decade. Major time on major things and minor time on minor things.

- Read books and listen to audiotapes. Read 6 books annually on your profession. Invest in books before you buy single-malt scotch. Just one new skill from each book means doing 6 things you don't do now.

- Do not sell products or services. Provide consultative and relationship marketing.

- Ask a non-buying client what you are doing wrong. You might be surprised with the answer. Then act on the response!

- Understand that many clients are bombarded with over 3000 ads and messages daily. That's correct – 3000! Messages are coming from the radio, television, newspapers, billboards, direct mail, sales people and more. These days, we are even deluged with "will work for food" signs. How are you going to stand out from the clutter? Be different!

Clients are always thinking I of 2 things when you walk through their door. They are: "I wonder how long this meeting is going to last," or "I am really going to like this person." Even if you are primarily a logical type sales person, remember that the first impression of you is made in 7 seconds! You better start with some emotion or you're dead in the water. Think: start with emotion, then logic, then to emotion, and so on. High energy and enthusiasm moves mountains.

Move From Left-Brain To Right-Brain Thinking

An example on how to move yourself from total left brain thinking into more creative thinking is as simple as this: On National Secretaries Day, typically we take our assistants to lunch and/or provide them with flowers. Don't do it! Instead, take them to lunch the week before "because you are more special than the others." Or give them an unexpected reward of the day off on National Secretaries Day.

I speak and consult on sales and marketing, and I am no slouch at it. My previous book "SELLING The Mother of All Enterprise" has been the #1 best seller for sales books according to groups such as Powell's Book Stores and American Society of Training and Development. (This book is the updated version of that book) Since I am so good at it, why do I have two marketing/PR agencies of my own? Two reasons. Firstly, nobody has all the answers. Secondly, I travel extensively and I provide tons of energy, logic, and creativity to my clients, and then I fly home. When I get home, I am brain dead. And then I go to the office for administrative purposes, and then I fly out for my next trip. I'm no different than you are — all of us need help.

To summarize, most sales are made from those that utilize right brain thinking. Most people base their purchasing decisions from the right side. Two competitors selling building materials or hot dogs – one of them will win the majority of the battles. Why? Almost always, one of them displays excitement, sells creatively, performs unheard of services, sees and paints things differently, and balances all of this with logical attributes such as time management and availability.

Use both sides of the brain, but focus on the right side. See things as they are and ask, "why not?" See things as they are and ask, "why?" Use just one side of the brain, and you will drive employees and clients mad and keep your wallet thin. Use both sides to their fullest, and watch what happens. Use both sides that you have been blessed with, or you will lose the side you abuse.

Using both sides will enable you to answer the question, "Is anybody happier because I passed this way?" Focus on that question because the #1 reason that people buy from a particular sales person is: they just like the sales person! That's a no-brainer.

CHAPTER TWELVE

Close The Sale And Keep The Client

Affirming the sale. Confirming the agreement. Sealing the deal. However you want to state it, getting the order or closing the sale is the bottom line in the sales process. If selling is the *Mother of All Enterprise*, closing the sale is winning a crucial battle that leads to winning the war.

With so much on the line, no wonder closing is something that makes many sales representatives tense. Their tension usually makes the client tense and suddenly the whole deal is on shaky ground. The closing process must be as smooth and effortless as the courtship. For that to happen, you must plan your closing visit carefully and move through the closing process without anxiety for you or your customer. It can be done, if you have paved the way by doing things that make closing a natural and easy conclusion to the pleasant process of exchange.

Before you ask for an order, your new customer must:

- Trust you
- Desire a relationship with you and the company you represent
- Be able to afford your products or services

- Be able to benefit from the use of your products or services

Please underline the third point. Note I stated the customer must be able to afford your offer. I did not say you had to have the best price. When the client wants to form a relationship with a particular sales person and the company he or she represents, getting the cheapest price is not foremost on the mind of the customer. Therefore, make price the last thing discussed.

Again, do not begin selling your offering until you have established a rapport with the client. That is, you must give prospects a reason to listen to you and get interested in what you have to present. Remember, studies show people are motivated to listen to someone talking by the following factors:

- 8% by the information presented
- 31 % by how information is verbalized
- 61% by nonverbal stimuli (how information is presented)

Combine factors two and three and you'll note 92 percent of a person's decision to listen to a sales presentation is made not by the information that is presented, but by how it is presented! Knowing this should be ample motivation to convince you to look your best, be prepared and exhibit enthusiasm or emotion when you are meeting with customers and prospects.

Nothing sells like enthusiasm. There, I said it again! Clients are able to quickly determine which sales representatives truly love what they do and believe in their products. Customers perceive they will receive exceptional after-the-sale service from the sales people who are genuinely enthusiastic. So remember, nothing gets customers involved in the process like excitement from the sales representative. Guess who has the responsibility for creating excitement? You! Don't think for a second you can count on the client to get you excited about what you do for a living.

Emotions Play A Big Role In Purchasing Decisions

In the end, most buying decisions are based on emotional factors. Purchasing decisions are justified later with logical reasoning. For example, every car I have purchased was bought for emotional reasons. If a car dealer had spent his time telling me about how many gallons of gasoline the car would hold and features of the engine, I probably would get bored in the process and leave the dealership before taking a test drive. Just let me sit in the car; or, let me take it for a test drive. If I like the way it feels and how I perceive myself behind the wheel, the sale is probably done. I'm an easy sell. I do, however, spend a little bit of time after the sale has been completed trying to come up with logical, practical reasons for the purchase. Sometimes I can, and sometimes I cannot. Emotionally, I just wanted the automobile and I bought it.

So, always show the customer a high energy level during the entire closing visit and try to understand the emotional factors playing on the buyer's purchasing decision. If you are overly assertive, only a small percentage of clients will be offended. If they do object to it, you can respond by saying, "I may be a little excited, as I genuinely want you for a customer. I am sorry." If you were the client and heard that, what would you say?

Remember to control the amount of talking you do. Ask questions such as, 'Will this help?" or "Will this improve?" and other pertinent questions that position you as a problem solver.

Be Prepared To Get The Big "NO"

Get ready for the word that even the most successful sales people often hear, "no." It is worth repeating; "no" is never final. It takes many "no's" to learn what it takes to get a "yes." Actually, studies show a potential customer will say "no" 5-6 times before they will say "yes."

Eighty percent of all sales are closed after the fifth contact. This is especially true if the customer must change vendors to do business with a new provider.

Overcoming Objections

With each objection, each turn down, ask the prospect the question, "How do you mean?" Then, be silent. "No" usually means, "you haven't convinced me yet." I picked up the use of the question, "How do you mean?" from Brian Tracy, a professional speaker, many years ago. I have probably utilized it thousands of times since and found it helps get to the bottom of what the client is thinking and has not revealed about what is preventing the sale. "No, no, no, no, no." Turn downs happen. It may be price, a strong relationship with another vendor or one of a dozen other reasons. Don't take it personally. I encountered a "no" the week I was writing this chapter. It turned out the vendor from whom the prospect was purchasing similar services was an in-law. In most similar cases, the relative always wins. Smart people understand, as quickly as possible, that the "no, thank you" phrase will be heard often. Just walk away and go on to the next prospect who will appreciate your offerings. Remember, however, the relative may fall out of favor or out of the family, leaving you an opening to do business at a future date. Check in annually with prospects you are not actively working but would like to convert to a customer one day.

Before giving up, find out which "no" is the critical one. Is it no confidence, no need, no money, no authority, or no urgency? When you do find out what is behind the "no" you can assess your next move. If the objection is impossible to overcome, move on to the next prospect and don't take the turn down as a personal failure.

When Price Is The Problem

Sometimes price is the barrier. When a client asks about my fees early in the visit, I respond with the phrase, "Can I save some more good news for later?" Sometimes when I hear, "Your fee is too high," I like to repeat it back with a question. "My fee of... is too high?" Then, I become silent so the prospect will respond to my question, which enables me to learn exactly why he feels my fee is not in line.

Many buyers know that a request for dirt-cheap prices will

fluster a sales representative. When a client puts too much pressure on you for unreasonable prices, you might respond by stating, "to meet your budget, let's decide which options you would like to leave off the order."

Another good response to hesitation because of price is to state, "We have found it is easier to justify price one time than to apologize for quality forever," or "It is usually better to pay a little more than you planned and get what you expect, than to pay a little less than you should and be disappointed with what you get." Each response gets potential customers to think about value and not just about price.

Reluctance To Change

The objection most often heard by sales people is, "We are happy with our current supplier." When the prospect tells you this, ask the following question, "What are your standards for quality?" Usually, you will hear, "We demand top quality and on time delivery." Your next question could be, "Are those standards being met 100 percent of the time by your current vendor?" Very few things in life are 100 percent perfect, especially over a long period of time. That is why the above question is a good one to ask. It may cause the buyer to do an honest reflection on the service provided by the current vendor. In addition, you can't match apples with apples unless you know your competitor is doing a great job in all the areas, which make up the purchasing decision.

The Six Objections Rule

There are six objections that are usually posed by buyers in most industries. Here are the six reasons why prospects do not buy:

Wrong seller	Wrong product
Wrong price	Wrong time
Wrong sales technique	Never asked to purchase

Therefore, be prepared. Learn the standard objections, the

ones you expect to hear most often. That way you can rehearse your responses and plan to overcome each objection.

I once bought a suit. While they placed the chalk marks on the cuffs of the jacket and the trousers I asked, "Which tie do I get with this suit?" I was told the store did not give away ties with a suit purchase. I replied, "Oh, I never buy a suit without a free tie." I challenged the sales person just to see how he would handle the situation. In the end, I got the tie, which showed me they valued my business. I'll bet the clothing establishment is better prepared to deal with other challenges to last minute deal busters in the future.

Remember, most sales are closed only after overcoming objections. There are few sales that close without the sales person leaping over a few barriers. View objections as questions to be answered and problems that need solutions. Do not take objections as a complete rejection.

Listen Hard

When a grenade explodes, everyone in the immediate area is likely to hear the explosion. Only a few, however, hear the sound of the grenade pin being pulled. They are the ones who can anticipate the danger, run for cover, and survive the attack.

Listening is a process that goes against human nature. Most people would rather be heard than listen to others speak. Closing a sale will be easier if you listen aggressively and learn from the exchange of information. Don't stop listening and begin analyzing before you have heard what the prospect really has to say. Instead, listen to the entire exchange and then repeat back the major points to the client. This shows you are paying attention and you thoroughly understand everything that was said to you.

I am the perfect example of a man who often doesn't listen when I should. Here's a story to illustrate the point. My wife and I flew to Nashville where I was scheduled to speak at a convention. The day before the convention, my daughter drove from Memphis to Nashville to visit us. The four-hour drive to Nashville in conjunction with several hours spent with us left my daughter very tired. She decided not to make the four-hour drive back to Memphis until the following day. My daughter had not planned to spend the night, so she arrived without her contact lens container and change of clothes.

She was in the bathroom of the hotel room when I asked her to come out so I could go in for just a few minutes before running downstairs to meet a client. On the way out of the bathroom, she said something like, "Dad, there are two glasses of water on the sink. Don't move them or drink from them because my contacts are in them." I heard her say something, but because I was thinking about the client downstairs, the entire message didn't register. I went into the bathroom and closed the door and before leaving I drank one of the glasses of water! She asked me later if I had heard her tell me about her contact lenses. It seemed vaguely familiar, but I hadn't really heard what she said. I was not an active listener. I was not giving her communication adequate attention or respect.

Listening is an activity essential to understanding the nature of and solutions to objections. Closing the sale is not cleverly overcoming objections. In reality, it is resolving concerns that are preventing the customer from placing the order. When the customer states an objection, you may want to respond, "I understand your position, but if I may explain..." Usually a good exchange of information and questions will follow which may even lead to another objection. Keep listening and overcome each objection, one by one, and you eventually will hear the real reason the customer is reluctant to buy. Usually there is only one essential barrier to overcome and eventually you will get to it if you keep probing.

Keep asking the right questions and keep listening carefully. To illustrate the point, let me tell a story I heard recently:

A person asked a stranger, "Does your dog bite?" The

reply from the stranger was "no." As the person bent over to pat the dog on the head, the dog promptly bit him on the hand. "I thought you said your dog did not bite," cried the man who had just been bitten. The stranger replied, "That's not my dog."

Target your questions so they will give you meaningful responses; responses that will help you understand what stands in the way of the sale. You may hear, "I want to think it over." When you do, respond with, "Great, what specifically do you want to think over?" Then be silent.

Out Of The Blue

You'll be surprised from time to time to get orders from accounts that at one point seemed almost impossible to close. These orders usually come in because the customer finally feels you are trustworthy, or has become dissatisfied with the current supplier. Almost every customer wants one thing, reassurance a new supplier will deliver as promised. To provide adequate reassurance, use words customers like to hear, such as "you, new, service, and profits." Again, provide plenty of referral letters from other customers that have purchased from you and are satisfied with your offering. Your effort may result in a surprise order months later.

Change Direction

Newt Gingrich served as a United States Congressman and as the House Minority Leader. We met as members of the Jaycees when we were both 29 years old. Newt asked me to serve as his finance chairman when he first ran for Congress. Newt had no political experience. Nevertheless, he felt he could serve constituents of his Congressional district better than the current Congressman, who was the most senior Democrat elected from the exclusively Democratic state of Georgia. Newt became the first elected Republican Congressman or Senator from Georgia since the Civil War. His victory wasn't easy.

During the campaign, we decided one of the first campaign

events would be a major neighborhood gathering in my backyard. Because I had a high profile in the community and a "go-getter" personality, we were both confident I could gather a large number of people to the event. We made plans for a few hundred people. The big shock came when absolutely no one attended. Rather than sulk, I began knocking on doors in the neighborhood that very night to ask why the neighbors had not come. I heard responses such as, "Our parents and grandparents always voted Democratic, and we have decided to continue the tradition."

I learned an important lesson from that dismal failure. I set up for a few hundred people without asking any of the neighbors prior to the event if they would come. I just pushed forward with positive expectations. Not everything, however, works out as hoped or planned. If I had visited the neighbors early and learned what they were really thinking, my approach would have been very different.

I also learned from that experience the importance of doing my homework. We had a great "product," but people in my neighborhood were not ready to buy it. Confidence in yourself and your product is one thing, but when the client is not receptive to exploring other options, there will not be a chance to make a sales presentation, let alone a sale.

After we regrouped, we asked the constituents questions about their concerns, listened extremely carefully and then offered a suggestion. I asked them to come to our next town meeting and "fire off" their best questions to Newt. Defeat is final only if you surrender, if you give up. We learned, we got better and Newt ultimately won the election by winning the respect of his constituents. There was a day when it seemed impossible. But, it wasn't. We learned from our initial mistakes and restructured the campaign to address the needs and concerns of the voters.

Use Creativity To Close The Sale

Creativity in sales can set you apart from the competition and help you develop proposals best suited to the needs, systems and problems of the customer. The following story illustrates the effectiveness of creativity. A client of mine flew cross-country to meet a prospective employer for a job interview. He was offered the job, but did not give the employer a definite response before catching a flight back home. Once home, he found the prospective employer had shipped a box of business cards to him with his name, title and all the pertinent information on the card! In other words, the employer used a creative method to let the recruit know they expected his answer to be "yes."

Using creativity in the sales process will bring in more accounts than just explaining over and over the features and benefits of your offering. Try to develop one or two things to use in closing a sale that might border on being considered outrageous in your industry. For example, when I was in the food industry, I provided sales training as a bonus to my customers. How many of my competitors do you think offered sales training to their customers and prospects? None.

Once I joined John, one of our sales representatives, on a sales call to a prospect in Portland, Oregon. For months, the prospect kept promising John he would place an order. During the visit, he told John, "I keep forgetting you." To me, that meant John had not done anything extraordinary during his sales calls that would make the prospect remember him and his products. He had not accomplished the most important first step in sales — getting the prospect to remember who you are and what you sell. Obviously John also had done nothing to excite the prospect and encourage him to buy.

John and I walked outside the client's facility and stood on their front porch. I asked John if he knew the date of the prospect's birthday. He didn't, so I suggested he go in and see the receptionist to get the information. The receptionist replied that she did not know because she had just started, but she went to check the records and came back and told John, "I'm glad you asked. His birthday is tomorrow!"

It was very late in the day so John and I hastily jumped in the car and went to the closest shopping mall. Soon we discovered how tough it is to shop for someone about, which you know little or nothing. To this point, John had discovered nothing of a personal nature about the client. So, shopping for someone without knowing anything about his or her interests or hobbies was tough.

Out of the corner of my eye, I spotted a vendor that took instant photos and through a computer process, the photos were printed on a woven calendar that was approximately 24 inches wide and 36 inches long. The calendar was designed to hang on the wall. I encouraged John to get his photo taken for the calendar. John was a little shy and said he did not want to participate. I convinced John to do it by sitting with him for the photo. The photo was printed on the calendar, rolled up and placed in a tube. We delivered it the same afternoon to the receptionist and asked her to give it to the client with the attached birthday card.

When we returned for the next appointment, the first thing we noticed was the calendar on the wall. The prospect pointed to the calendar and stated, "There is no way I can ever forget about you two, now!" He thought it was funny. We walked out with our first order. So, utilize creativity to your advantage. Make yourself different, even outrageous, if that's what is takes to get the order.

Ask For The Business

Above all, be sure to ask for the business. For some strange reason, many sales people never ask for the order. They just drift through the conversation and leave. What a total waste of everyone's time. Studies conducted by Chris Hegarty, a professional speaker and consultant, show 65 percent of all sales representatives do not attempt to bring closure with a client. Think about it. Sixty-five percent never ask for an order!

Some sales trainers advise sales people to resort to games and tricks to close the sale or to utilize "power closes." I don't believe those tactics serve the sales person over the long run. What I believe works best in sales are excellent people skills, coupled with sensible and ethical sales and marketing techniques.

If you have completed all of the minimum requirements in the selling process, and added a few creative approaches of your own, all that is left to do is to ask for the order. Most qualified prospects will deliver the order sooner or later.

By minimum requirements, I mean the prospect must need and want what you have to offer, have the means and power to make the purchase, be open to the change required to buy from you now and want to establish a relationship with you and your business. If these requirements are in place, you must recognize the opportunity and do whatever it takes to get the customer to place the order.

The selling process should be fun. It is a task in which you get paid for bringing helpful products and services to people who need them. The more value you bring to your customers, the greater the sales and the higher your resulting income. Therefore, the value you deliver can easily be measured by your income. To me, income is a yardstick measuring how well you are doing. Income is not something to gloat over nor complain about. It is just a yardstick, a measurement of the results of your efforts.

Keep Your Clients

Let's assume for a moment you have many clients. Clients are not just customers; they are business partners involved in a long-term relationship. Continued success is dependent upon not losing the clients you have. Clients are not easily acquired.

Once you build an established client base, do not take on new tasks and objectives that might cause you to ignore your existing clients. That is the downfall of many potentially great sales people. Return telephone calls fast. Clients call for a reason, so find out why they called and take care of their requests promptly.

Personally, I do not like a business telephone system with call waiting. I believe it is rude to make a call to a client or to receive a call from a client only to place the individual on hold in order to talk to someone else. To me, that's extremely unprofessional. Instead of spending a few dollars for call waiting, spend a few dollars for voice mail. Voice mail enables you to communicate with confidence on the telephone knowing a voice mail system will retrieve any other inbound calls. You can return calls later, when you can give each caller your complete attention.

Always stay in touch with your current and past clients by telephone, post card, letter or personal visit. Never ignore an existing client or they may begin to ignore you. Keep bringing value to the client on a regular basis. Never stop cultivating your client. If you stop, someone else will catch you with your guard down and walk away with an order you should have obtained.

One of the nicest things you can do for a client is acknowledge how much you appreciate their business. Telephone to say, "Joe or Mary, I'm calling just to tell you how much I appreciate you as a client. Please think about how I can better service you and whenever you think of anything I could do better, just call." By acknowledging the business they provide and by staying in touch with clients, they will know you are not taking advantage of them or taking their business for granted.

Not For The Weak Or Faint Of Heart

If you think achieving success in sales is too tough, then ask yourself, "Why?" Why try hard? Why use any new ideas from this book? Why work hard to achieve success? Well, why not? When launching the Apollo program, John Kennedy said, "We choose to go to the moon, not because it is easy, but because it is hard."

Why not decide to act on your goals now, decide to go after all that life has to offer? Joe DiMaggio was asked why he placed such a high value on playing quality baseball everyday. He replied, "There is always some kid in the stands who is seeing me for the first or the last time. I owe him by best." To be on top of your game, you owe your customers your very best, everyday.

No single individual or company has a long-term advantage. None can coast. If you are not in the top position, you can be. You must, however, make changes in the way you do things. There's good and bad news in this message. The good news — you will receive rewards for your positive actions. The bad news — if you view it that way — the process goes on forever. You can never rest on your laurels.

All professional baseball players, football players and basketball players must go to training camp every year and workout all year long to stay in playing condition. A certain percentage of them lose their spot on the roster each season to someone with more talent or more desire. That's why I really like the selling process. It's like sports. Each encounter is a game that can be won or lost. Playing is rewarding in itself, but chalking up wins provides tremendous personal satisfaction, as well as financial rewards.

Teddy Roosevelt summed it up extremely well:

> *"It is not the critic who counts; not the man who points out how the strong man stumbled, or where the doer of deeds could have done better. The credit belongs to the man who is actually in the arena; whose face is marred by dust and sweat and blood; who strives valiantly; who errs and comes short again and again; who knows the great enthusiasms, the great devotions, and spends himself in a worthy cause; who at best knows in the end*

*the triumph of high achievement; and who at the worst
if he fails, at least fails while daring greatly; so that his
place shall never be with those cold and timid souls who
knew neither victory nor defeat."*

Teddy Roosevelt made it sound like war. It is a war out there.
It calls for strong and dedicated individuals who have a love
affair with what they do and have a desire to bring value to
others, in addition to quality goods and services. The old
business adage, "nothing happens until somebody sells something
to someone," is basic. In business, selling is fundamental to
survival. Strong organizations thrive on the ability of their sales
force to sell.

Thinking about Lt. Clebe McClary keeps me on my toes.
Clebe was similar to many young men who came out of high
school and college in the middle 1960s. Viet Nam was yet to get
really ugly and many of our generation wanted to do what our
fathers and grandfathers had done, which was to serve honorably
in the armed forces. It seemed the right thing to do. Clebe
McClary went the full distance. He asked to join the Marine
Corps, he asked to be an officer and he asked for duty in Viet
Nam. He got all three requests.

On a mountaintop in Viet Nam, he and his men became
embroiled in heavy combat. There were seven dead and six
wounded when Clebe McClary called for a helicopter rescue
mission. The initial transmission came back, "It's too foggy; we
cannot take off yet." His reply was, "Never mind then, because
in another hour the only ammo we will have is rocks to throw
down the hill." Another helicopter unit picked up his transmission
and took off on the rescue mission.

Clebe McClary was doing what he was paid to do, what he
was trained to do and what he said he wanted to do-be a military
leader. He was doing his best to command this unit, direct fire
and bring aid to the wounded. Later, when helicopters came to
take Clebe McClary and his men out, he discovered part of his

arm was missing. Clebe McClary was too busy giving to others to take notice of himself.

They saved Clebe McClary's life. When it came time to send him to Japan for additional surgery, a plaque was sent to him from his comrades and commanding officer, which read:

> *The world is full of give and take, but very few give all that it takes.*

TOP GUN
LEADERSHIP
AND
MANAGEMENT

CHAPTER THIRTEEN

Mastering Change

Do you remember when we were younger, we used to run and jump into the ocean, lake or pool? And what do we do now? We stick our toes in first to see if the water is comfortable or "safe" enough for us. You can't afford to be neither safe nor comfortable in your profession. That equals the town of Conclusion – the place where you got tired of thinking.

As individuals in a fast-changing world, we should never fall into the career and corporate killer of thinking "I/we are okay". You must buy into the fact that to stay ahead of a competitive market, the change internally must accelerate more so than the external changes every industry faces. The President must improve as does the Sales Manager. If they don't, who will?

It is still a people business so let me ask 5 questions regarding people that might create some soul-searching.

Managing or Leading?

Is your management team managing or leading? Most people respond in quantum leaps to a leader as compared to them just doing what a manager wants done. Leaders set the tone for greatness from everyone else. A role model.

A client's employee told me his boss "doesn't have ulcers... he's a carrier." So goes the boss, so goes the crew.

Top Gun?

Do you have one salesperson who is in the top 2% of all salespeople in your industry? Are 20% of your salespeople in the top 10% in the industry? If not, what help do they need? I have seen salespeople who were at the bottom go to the top in 1 to 2 years. They just need to be trained and educated in sales greatness. Remember, half the salespeople you know... are below average.

Just as 99% of lawyers give the rest of them a bad name, many "salespeople" fit in the same category. They just don't know what they don't know yet.

Something New?

What did everyone do last week that they had never done before? If someone's "new thing" bombed, be sure to compliment them for trying and encourage them to keep doing new things. Failure must be encouraged because whenever a person tries new things, they won't always go perfectly. How was your first French kiss? How was your first attempt at parallel parking? Probably not too wonderful, but you got better at it with persistence.

Value?

What new "joy and value" factor did each salesperson incorporate into a client proposal? If you want your revenues to change, you might need to change the way you sell. Think creatively. Think like this: "what am I personally going to do so that they **need** me and **want** me?"

When I hear salespeople talk, talk and talk, I know the potential client is thinking. "It's hard to believe he beat out 1,000,000 other sperm." Talk less and think more – before you ever make the visit.

Service?

What service do you offer that blows clients out of their chairs? Should you provide them with sales and management education? There's no downside there. What service can you offer that no one else in the industry offers? Then, add a second service.

Creativity and Innovation Required

I read recently that the American Management Association asked 500 CEO's "what must one do to survive in the 21st century?" The top answer was "practice creativity and innovation". You must encourage **everyone** to challenge everything in the way they do things – and expect it on a regular basis.

Some examples of a little creativity just to get you started:

- When a client is way overdue with payment, you could add to their statement: "we have already done more for you than your own mother. We have carried you for 10 months". Or, "Why do our bills travel through the mail at twice the speed of your check?"

- When it is appropriate to send flowers, don't do it. Send cactus because they just don't die. You will be there forever. A gift that "sticks". I gave a 2-inch cactus plant to a businesswoman 21 years ago. It is now 23 inches high (they grow 1 inch per year). She can't forget me.

- I was field-training a salesperson and we visited a potential client that he had never earned an order from yet. The client said "John, I just keep forgetting you".

We left and standing outside, I asked the salesperson when the client's birthday was. He didn't know (not good) so he went inside and found that the birthday was the next day! We drove to a nearby mall and there it was. An entrepreneur had a business of taking a person's photo and scanned it on a long woven calendar. I told John to sit down and make a funny face for the photographer. He cowered so I told him I would sit with him. I put my two fingers up, feather-style at the back of his head, and John waved. The next day the calendar was on the client's wall. He couldn't forget us. John got his first-ever order the next week.

When you're out, how far out can you be? Be far out to get way in. Boring is out and creativity was – and still is in.

- I attended a staff meeting with an aviation client in Albuquerque and I looked outside and saw a 747 that was given to FAA for inspection training. I said to a salesperson "go get on the rear wing and get your photo taken". Another person said, "FAA would never let us do that". I said, "go call them". The salesperson wound up getting his photo, on the wing, in his business attire for a post card that said "when I said anytime and anyplace, I meant it!" I also got him to have a photo taken in a Santa Claus suit, on the wing, for his holiday cards.

This salesperson went from last place in the standings, to the top because he tried 100% of the logical and creative ideas I gave him. Not only did he have fun, but the clients loved his creativity and fun.

- Send telegrams to get a client's attention. Sound like old-school thinking? It's not. If 3 packages from Federal Express, UPS and Western Union landed on your desk, which one would you open first? You didn't think

Western Union was still around? That's why you use them!

- Any chief can take an assistant to lunch on National Executive Assistants Day. Wouldn't it be better to take your "great one" to lunch a month before? Taking her/him on the same day everyone else takes their assistant to lunch is not that special. Do it just because it is the right thing to do for a valuable person. You will be the winner. A day without sunshine is like... night.

- Instead of saying to a client "let's do lunch", set up a hot air balloon ride with breakfast. Get photos taken and put it in a frame for the client. Beats lunch at a Holiday Inn any day of the week. And get a "co-pilot" certificate in a frame also.

- Instead of buying all of your postage stamps from the post office, get your own stamps made with your photo. I race cars once in a while so my stamps feature me in a race-driving suit. Just a little attention-getter.

- Set up "Creativity Week" corporate-wide. Challenge your sales force to do 10 new things for 10 potential clients. Set up incentives for the most creative ideas such as 1st, 2nd, and 3rd place, but also award a bonus to the person that failed, even though the idea was ingenious. Set up the same incentives internally. Offer monetary ($) change for change.

  We have thoughts about someone like "if you gave him a penny for his thoughts, you would get change". Well, challenge them to think more creatively and watch how most will surprise you.

- Have some hard-to-see potential clients? Get an author

of a book to place a personal statement along with the author's autograph. The inscription could simply read "To: John Smith. Jane asked me to autograph this book for you... I hope you enjoy it. Bill Blades." Many of the potential clients will call you before you call them.

Work, work, work is what we are taught to do. I enjoy working with organizations to get them to S... L... O... W... down so that they can creatively think about changing the way they do things. Many people don't think – they just do things out of habit. One client recently had a blank look. I asked him what he was thinking about. He said, "I just got lost in thought. It was unfamiliar territory."

We drive to work the same way every day. We make sales calls like we did last year. We manage the same way without excitement. Think "new" and "creativity" every week. The #1 thing we have to offer to our clients and to our employees is our brain, but we often don't take the quiet time, the thinking time, to get out of the box.

It is an ever-changing world and our internal change better be ahead of the curve and creating the change or it may become too late to catch up. Eagles soar and the weasels get sucked up into jet engines.

The sooner you fall behind, the more time you will have to catch up. It's a no brainer choice – no creativity needed.

CHAPTER FOURTEEN

Top Gun Leadership

What constitutes a great leader? That question is asked of me as often as "what makes a great sales person?" Both answers would be more than a mouthful, but I will provide you with a list of areas I believe are most important to remember.

Culture

Leaders are the spearhead for the corporation's culture. Fanaticism has its place here. Anything less than a culture that calls for greatness in everything you do will not work.

Planning

The sales and marketing plan and the business plan should be reviewed monthly to ensure that we stay on track and *beat* self-imposed deadlines. Focus intently on sales, particular clients and development of your human resources.

Time Utilization

Major time should be invested in major things. There are two majors — your group and your clients. How many days a month do you spend with clients, listening to them? How many days a month do you spend with your group? Then consider, how many days should you be spending with each?

Think

Instead of just doing, leaders must take the necessary quiet time to think about new ways of doing things. A Phoenix-based aircraft parts company has quiet rooms where the employees can go to read self-improvement books and magazines. Everyone needs to be challenged to more fully utilize his or her brain – to think creatively.

Feedback

How do your peers think of you? How do your subordinates feel about you? Ask and see if there are any surprises to your self-perception. Get a management personality profile run on you so that you better understand yourself and the image you project.

Failing

I believe we learn more from failures than successes. Yet, most leaders have not encouraged their people to fail more. Failing usually comes form doing new things. Did everyone on your staff do one new thing last week? Should they have?

Proactive

Leaders will hardly ever have all of the information they need for a decision. When you wait for all the details, your final decision may be too late. Don't worry about being 100 percent correct in 100 percent of the cases.

Creativity

I have creative ideas that have helped a lot of clients become more successful. I have also provided some client with a bunch of ideas that were, less than spectacular. Encourage everyone to put every creative idea they have on the table. Defend an individual, if you must, if more than 50 percent of his ideas are duds. With the duds, come the gems.

Appreciation

You have a lot of quiet, behind-the-scenes people who do not get a lot of attention – and probably do not want any. What they do want and need is a little appreciation. Just a cup of coffee with one new person a week will pay dividends. Listen to them, because they know more about their sector than you do.

Fun

Is it the most fun place in the town to work? When people love what they do, you get better performance.

Giving

Leaders gain respect and power by sharing their time and talents and not taking credit from others. Give to get.

Listening

Leaders ask tons of questions and listen intently to every word. Introverts do not usually say much. When they do, hang on to every word.

Cutting-edge

What unheard-of service do you offer that no one else does? Keep the edge on your group to provide suggestions for low-cost value-added services that will create a niche in the marketplace. Think about a service that creates a partnership with clients.

Succession

If you ran into a telephone pole tomorrow, who would take your place? Never let yourself be indispensable and never let anyone be so either. Put in everyone's job description that they must recruit, select and train their replacement.

Intuition

Experienced leaders, through many victories and defeats, have learned to stay tuned to their intuition. When doubt crawls in and your "gut feeling" tells you something is wrong, it probably is.

Courage

Many leaders do not tell their chief the truth. Silence is not golden — it is cowardice.

Mission

Everyone needs a reminder as to our mission statement. Eat, sleep and breathe it. Make it real. Get everyone involved. It is a vital responsibility that is often seen as trivial. It is not.

Resources

Leaders understand that most people have not been stretched enough. Provide targeted training and education and you earn the right to raise expectations from everyone.

Re-energize

Leaders always keep the edge on everyone. They often utilize the word "absolute," so that everyone understands that anything less than an all-out effort is intolerable. Let them see the fire in your belly from time to time. Then furnish unexpected rewards to those who came early, stayed late, came in on Saturdays, and to those that spoke out. Give them a day off, a dinner for two or whatever.

Then treat yourself to a similar reward, because real leaders deserve it.

CHAPTER Fifteen

Top Gun Sales Management

Approximately 85% of all managers in North America become managers without the prior education to become one – I'm sure you can imagine how well that goes in many cases.

The traits that I see needing improvement most of the time are:

CEO Is Too Easy

Leadership is sometimes hard and sometimes soft, but I find that most CEO's are far too easy on the next layer down. The various reasons include not gutsy enough, don't know how to counsel professionally and even favoritism. Tell them the truth when you should do. If you don't, it's called cowardice.

Then the executive group might do the same with everyone else. It starts way up there.

Communications

Whether in our personal or business lives, the first thing that causes divisiveness is a break down in communications. Communication either just stops or it becomes short and to the point. No coffee with it, no sincerity and very little contact with the person.

Seven of 10 people that lose their jobs do so from some form of communications. Remember it is not what you say, but how you say it.

If a co-worker stops talking to you, you should immediately visit the person and ask if you have done something wrong – ask for the truth. Also, remember that people are more relaxed when they are either laying down or sitting over a beverage or meal. Since you don't want the person laying down in your office, I suggest you conduct the meeting over coffee. Even Lipton employees have meetings with coffee.

Absolutes

Once a decision has been made, share with your group that "this is an absolute. By that, I mean that failure is not an option."

From that day forward, using the word "absolute" will have a profound effect. From Eisenhower's D-Day "we go", John Kennedy's "we will place a man on the moon and bring him back safely to earth" or General Schwarzkopf's briefing on Iraq "we will cut its head off", there was no question as to an all out effort.

What is the one big absolute you need to share with your group – now?

Micro-Managing

If you want to kill creativity and enthusiasm, don't let your group "get on with it" without your placing your approval on every piece of the puzzle. Micro-managing is similar to the newspaper headline that read "Red Tape Holds up New Bridge." Oh, the mediocre people will not mind your meddling, but the really good ones will hate it – and probably leave you. It's smart to follow-up, but dumb to control everything carefully.

Brain Challenge

Most of us can do our jobs with one arm. Even with one arm and one leg. Yet, the number one thing that managers, and their staff, have to offer is their brain. Yet, I hardly ever see anyone really thinking enough? They are too busy just "doing". And very little creativity comes out by high-speed motion. Slow it down by taking at least four hours a week just to think.

I suggest you challenge every person that reports to you to provide a monthly report. It can include the following topics: what am I doing that I should not be doing, what am I not doing that I should be doing and a minimum of 1 high quality, creative idea to boost sales, teamwork, morale and whatever else that might be a challenge. And, help them implement the suggestions.

1-on-1 Development

Every person reporting to you can become a minimum of 25% more effective. Often, they don't know how to, so it becomes your responsibility to pinpoint their areas to improve and arrange for the assistance necessary.

If the improvements require an outside resource, the improvements can become either an expense or a great investment. It will be a cost if you do not hold the individual accountable for acting on the new skills she received. Hold her accountable and it will become a great investment.

Personal Growth

I am talking about you here. Your dedication to personal growth earns you the right to ask others to improve.

The first area to conduct an assessment on is in communications. It is still the number on of the biggest reasons why very bright leaders flounder. Ask a few people who will tell you the truth, how well you are doing in communications.

Then, what is the next area to assess? Then what's after that? Even with you, it is still called continuous improvement. Even school teachers seek improvement according to a recent headline that read "Sex Education Delayed, Teachers Request Training".

Time Utilization

Time is our real currency and we need to treat it as such. The average executive is interrupted 50 to 80 times daily. Let's just use 50 and say each interruption is only 5 minutes. That's 4 hours that is lost daily. We are paid to think and you can not effectively do so if you don't block out quiet time. I suggest you pick certain hours where no interruptions are allowed just to think.

My best thinking time is when I first wake up in the morning because there is nothing else to interfere with my thoughts. Idea: stay home one day a month just to think and plan. No interruptions. It's the same as going to the office on Saturday for 4 hours. You get 2 days of work done. Right?

Favorites

One of the worst mistakes a manager can make is making a bad hiring decision. And, then letting that person remain on the payroll is bad for overall morale.

The only thing worse than employee turnover is when there is none of it when there should be. I recently suggested that an employer discharge an employee for non-performance. He said, "Bill, I would, but I am afraid he would go to work for our competitor." Duh. "That's where you want him to go," I replied. The CEO liked him, regardless of performance.

Even Nordstrom's marks down slow moving merchandise – and fast. And, it doesn't matter how much they like the outfit. Not one else does, so move it at any price.

Culture

Some see this as a fluffy area...an option. It is anything, but that. It is almost everything.

The best cultures call for the business to be the most fun place in town to work. When work becomes fun, teamwork improves, productivity is elevated, turnover is reduced and creativity is unleashed. And, of course, sales are elevated.

A quick check to perform – is everyone eating, sleeping and breathing your mission statement? I have had more than one CEO, in the last few years, who could not tell me his mission statement. When the CEO doesn't embrace greatness, no matter the size of the organization, the deathbed is already being packed ready for shipment.

Conclusion

We often use the words management and leadership as if they were the same. They are not. For you military veterans, think Drill Sergeant and General. For you non-military veterans, the difference there is one barks orders while the other thinks, plans, strategizes and rallies troops.

Don't stop payment on your reality check. I suggest you rate yourself on the above 10 skill sets and figure out which ones you will begin to attack immediately. And, don't forget to be totally honest – another leadership trait.

CHAPTER SIXTEEN

Coaching

In baseball, you can't become a manager unless you are a great coach. The same is true in business. I have never met a businessperson that could not improve their personal effectiveness by at least 25% — many by 50%.

Growth

A manager must be growing at a faster rate than his own group. He has then earned the right to expect improved productivity. This method is preferred much more than him thinking he is okay, and "telling his people they are not doing their jobs well enough. Wise men learn from fools more than fools learn from wise men.

Truthful

I find that most managers hold back in telling the truth. They are afraid that the truth might hurt the individual. The opposite is true so I call this for what it is — cowardice. I conduct 1-on-1 developmental sessions and I ask the manager "what are the top 3 things you would like this person to get better at?" This way, the truth gets put on the table in a nice and easy way, but

I too often hear the individual respond "you (the manager) never told me that before." After we get that settled, we reach agreement with the individual for the specified improvements.

Coaching

Some managers don't know how to provide high-quality coaching and it proves to be very destructive. They do not know what they do not know yet. They must understand that it isn't what you say, but how you say it. Let's call it "style." I suggest, in most cases, that dosages of humor helps because it creates a fun, non-threatening environment. To be pleasing to people is a big step with persuading them to your point of view. I also suggest that coaching be done, in certain cases, over beverages or even a meal. People are most relaxed and receptive over a meal/beverage or when lying down. If you are not a couch-type psychologist, only one of those is an option.

Keywords also help. They can include "I want to help you improve, get closer to your real potential, etc." You can also use " I want you to know how I feel" and " what I am thinking" versus "here's how it is." Talk to them as you would like to be talked to. In a democracy, it's okay to tell someone how you feel or think. It's democratic in a business setting also.

At the end of the meeting, you must agree to methods and dates for follow-up. In most cases, it is smart to touch base the following day to get a "reading" of the person's mindset, attitude and their initial progress. Then, follow up weekly.

Performance Appraisal

An area that many managers are ill-equipped to do a good/great job at is with Performance Appraisals. Too many are still conducted as a one-way session... a "boss with a subordinate." Leadership is a two-way street... that is, loyalty, respect and care starts with you. You are not just the boss... you are a servant. There is a big difference between the two. Your attitude, at the beginning of the appraisal, will help determine the successful outcome.

The first thing to remember is that many people will tell you that they welcome criticism, but what they really want is praise. So, give them praise for the areas they will score well in. Then, share with them what they need to improve upon to further develop their career path. Then, another praise. It's like a sandwich: praise, then some meat, followed by another piece of praise. And don't utilize off-the-shelf position descriptions and measurements. They should be customized not just for your organization, but for the specific individual.

Remember to take care of a basic need in…. letting the individual know how important she is to the organization. Along with that important message, share how important it is that she displays growth in a current area that needs improving or a new area of responsibility. Share that she does not need to score 100% in every area. Tell her "if at first you don't succeed, destroy all the evidence that you tried." A little dosage of humor that is well – timed is helpful. Then, share "please come see me whenever you want to bounce your progress off of me, I would love to help you succeed." That send-off promotes trust, relationships and an open-style of communications.

A final point on coaching is to have one primary goal to reach at the conclusion of the session. Open the session with the stated goal and close it with the goal. Establish the agreement and agree on the key objectives to reach the goal. Be very clear. Newspaper headlines are not your role model for clear communications. Here's some headlines I shook my head over:
"Stud Tires Out"
"Panda Mating Fails – Veterinarian Takes Over"
"Prostitutes Appeal to Pope"
"Iraqi Head Seeks Arms"
"Eye Drops off Shelf"

The point is to make sure she doesn't return for a follow-up meeting to say, "oh, I didn't understand you to say that when we met." Ever heard that? Be clear and confirm it in writing. Leave nothing to chance.

Coaching skills often go amiss because the one doing the coaching usually has never received great coaching himself. Nor has he been educated to be a great coach. It would be like taking Sammy Sosa out of the line-up and making him the baseball club's manager the next day. It would be a fiasco just as corporations promote a salesperson to the position of V.P. of Sales without training and education to be a great V.P. of Sales. And the CEO wonders what is wrong with sales. Amazing.

Great coaching is as rare as my steaks. It's too bad because it hurts revenues – and peoples' lives.

CHAPTER SEVENTEEN

Vice President of Sales

Do you know of anyone who has a bachelor's degree in Vice-President of Sales? I don't either. So how do they become a great one? They seek out a mentor, a role model or consultant – and preferably all three. Why, to get better – because no one scores a 10 in every area. The 10 activities that the top 5% of all V.P.s of sales do, and do really well are:

Understanding Yourself

I am often asked to work with a client to help the salespeople improve their performance. I have a standard reply which is "I would be delighted to, but I need to start with you first." The sales chief must be growing at a faster rate than the people they lead. So goes the chief, so goes the troops. Seek the truth and act on it. It all starts and ends with you. Be honest with yourself.

Plan and Focus

Planning for the next 12 months will keep everyone focused on the main goals and objectives for the year. Always place the heaviest emphasis on two primary areas: your clients and your troops. Your people and clients – don't get side tracked with all the little "things" that chew up your time and results. Executives lose over 25% of their time on little things. Don't do it. Treat your time like it is currency.

Sales and Marketing Plans are a must. This is your blueprint for ever major activity for the year. Deadline dates must be applied to the majority of the items in the plan. The plan must be reviewed monthly with the purpose of meeting or beating the deadline dates. This eliminates corporate drift. The plane need not be fancy with color graphs and mundane date. Just include the major activities that you need to do for growing your group and your sales.

Your People

We say wonderful things like "people are our greatest asset", but do we live it? Most organizations, unfortunately, fail miserably. We invest funds for equipment and the like, but we look at training and education as a cost. It is just the opposite. Hold the group accountable for new sales skills they have acquired and your investment will pay dividends. And don't just provide classroom training. An abundance of 1-on-1 education works better. One person at a time.

Sales meeting should have several goals. The first meeting should be the best sales meeting the organization has ever experienced. The following sales meeting should then be the best one ever... and so on. I understand that making every sales meeting the best one is a tall order, but it is your responsibility.

The meeting should be charged with energy and activity. It should be a fun environment so that individuals look forward to coming. Next, be sure to provide training that is practical and targeted towards the group's needs. Remember that an abundance of product training does not turn an average performer into a great performer. Sales training is the priority followed by product training.

Again, the VP must hold the group accountable for the skills they learned at the sales meeting. If not, many people will leave the meeting and go into the field with old skills and habits. Monitor, monitor, monitor.

Your Clients

Nothing beats a Target Account Program. Identify those clients you want to initially obtain, those you want to increase revenues with and those you do not want to lose. Plan out the activities every department, and person, will do to boost your sales efforts with every Target Account. Lay it out by month for focus – and then monitor not just the year-to-date activities, but keep everyone on-target for the next 3 months. Be proactive.

Departmental Culture

You can choose a culture of being pretty good or great. One will equal pretty good results while the other will equal greatness. Is every staff member adhering to the corporate mission statement? Repeat. Everyone? Greatness will only be achieved when you hold everyone accountable for personal greatness. Remember, most people want to get better. Help them. They must be told the truth and provided with assistance and accountability. We tell our cherished loved ones what we feel and think. Love your staff also.

Motivation

This requires you to be both hard and soft. Be hard on them when you need to be and soft with them when you should. So, if a person is down, off course or lagging in results, get with it. What is each one of you going to do as soon as your 1-on-1 session is completed? Agree to it and monitor. By soft, I mean that praise and unexpected rewards should be given when deserved. You don't have to over-do it; just be sure to do it. Question: did you or any of your troops get too many pats on the back last week? Didn't think so. Do what is right when you should do. Not later.

Recruiting

Recruiting must be an ongoing process. You must continue recruiting when you do not need anyone. This helps you to select the right people by interviewing them at least 3 times to include an informal meeting at a restaurant. Recruiting only when you need someone is bad business. A rushed decision made because you urgently need a body will probably haunt you down the road. The V.P. of sales should get a personality profile processed on the individual and possibly utilize a consultant in one of the sessions.

I can't train the wrong people so you must invest in the resources to improve the caliber of your new-hires. Utilize a consultant for interviewing, have a personality profile (by sales profession) run on the candidate and figure out how you can get to the truth about the person. Why? Resumes are simply a paid advertisement and the majority of them have been enhanced to stretch the truth. Recruit when you do not need anyone and interview each candidate 2 to 3 times, dine with them, meet their significant others, get into their domicile. Be a tough sell and don't hire them just because you like them. Like many employers do.

High D

Most people are aware of the four primary personality styles which are "D" for dominant (the driver), "I" for influencer (the talker), "S" for steady (slow and sure) and "C" for compliant (everything must be perfect before acting).

To the point – high I people usually talk too much without results. High S people hardly ever get into high gear. High C individuals are in the wrong profession if they are in sales. It's more high D people that most organizations need. They get things done – and quickly. Good news. You can get their D score up with the proper education. Get the D score up and results go up. Hire high D people and help the others get their D score up. You won't recognize them in 6 months.

Delegation

I went into my last corporate position as V.P. of Sales and Marketing and the CEO and I shared an executive assistant. About 3 months later, the CEO said "you're the best delegator I have ever seen. She is much more productive then I ever dreamed of – you take her full-time and I will find someone new." He never delegated so she never knew how valuable she could be.

Get others to do more things, new things, and valuable things. Everyone. Then get out from out behind that computer screen – then get someone else to do it.

The Edge

Keep the edge on everyone – including yourself. Act on major things (people and clients) every day. Never let up. Never believe you and your group are good enough. You're not because you never arrive. What do you and your group need to get better at? Act on them. Now.

Pardon my bias, but the sales chief is the spark plug for not just the sales group, but for everyone. If you do not score a 9 or 10 in each of the above areas, get assistance. If you're not honest with yourself, I hope your CEO reads this – and will be.

To be successful, feel successful, said your father. Now, you hopefully know how wise he was.

ABOUT THE AUTHOR

Bill Blades, CMC, CPS, is the only one in history to serve as Chairman of both National Speakers Association Sales PEG and Institute of Management Consultants Marketing SIG. He is widely respected by his peers internationally as a leader in sales and sales management training and education.

He has been a leading salesperson, top regional sales manager, and a dynamic vice president of sales and management. He has spoken and consulted for hundreds of clients internationally — helping them to elevate leadership skills, to enhance a culture of greatness, to create world-class service, and to outsell their competitors.

CONSULTING SERVICES

Coaching for CEO's, Executives, Managers, and Sales Personnel

Focus for Effectiveness

Sales and Marketing Action Plans

Sales Training and Education

Leadership Training and Education

Time Utilization

Field Training

Corporate Culture/Teamwork Enhancement

Creativity to the Extreme

Proactive Solutions to Help Get On With it

1-on-1 Coaching

Personality Profiles by Profession

Position Descriptions/Measurement Devices

Recruiting and Interviewing Services

Speaking and Consulting for Your Clients

Client Focus Sessions

Speaking on all of the above topics

To Book Bill Blades

Please contact:
William Blades
Phone: 480-563-5355
Fax: 480-563-0515
email: bill@williamblades.com
www.williamblades.com

PRESENTATION TOPICS

Reenergizing The Organization for Greatness

This is a customized presentation that includes portions on leadership, corporate culture, internal and external service and sales. The flow is: leadership determines the culture – culture determines the level of internal services – internal services determine external services. Together, all of these factors equal more sales.

Selling – Being Different Makes The Difference: 200 Little Things That Create Big Successes

This seminar is loaded with hard-core business skills. No power closes or gimmicks – just skills that produce more business. This course can contain your choice of: organization, preparation, prospecting, first call, relationships, planning, momentum, creativity, and closing.

Selling – It's A Whole-Brainer: Learning To Use The Creative Side Of Your Brain

Learn to blend the creative side of your brain with the logical side to better sell your product or ideas. Most sales people talk about themselves, their products, their services and how competitive they will be. Naturally, this is pretty boring stuff. This program teaches how to ask the right questions, listen intently to learn and take great notes. Then apply creativity to the clients' basic needs, which will set you apart from the pack.

Power Up The Corporation: Creating A Culture Of Greatness

This program will help you define the key actions which will change the fundamental personality of your group and infuse new-found excitement about your mission. If it is the most fun place in town to work, productivity will increase, creativity comes from all over the organization, and recruiting gets easier. The culture must be one that calls for greatness from every individual.

PRESENTATION TOPICS (cont.)

Stand Out Or Sit Down: World Class Customer Service

Learn how to provide better service than any other competitor in your industry. Get your entire team to understand the business you're in is service. Most organizations talk about it while some figure out how to do everything they said they would do – and more. In addition, providing un-heard of services is the vital key to stand out.

Leaders Dream, Plan and Do: Preparing For Proactive Leadership

This program will help your managers boost productivity while building teamwork and enthusiasm. Includes: big picture thinking, dealing with deadlines, attention to details. Everyone looks to the leader as the role model, so the leader must understand that he or she is the spark plug. Give of yourself, care and nurture others and set a personal example for others to follow.

Other Topics Also Available:

Bill delivers tailored keynotes, breakouts and seminars.

To Book Bill Blades

Please contact:
>William Blades
>Phone: 480-563-5355
>Fax: 480-563-0515
>email: bill@williamblades.com
>www.williamblades.com

Testimonials

Deere & Company
I wanted to take this opportunity to thank you on behalf of our dealer organization for four terrific 'on target' presentations! The time you spent here at Deere & Company, along with the dealer visitations, helped to tailor your remarks. Thanks for a superb job... you met our expectations!
    – D.G. Noble, Director/Parts Marketing

Equipment Manufacturers Institute
On the evaluation form completed at the conclusion of the meeting, one person best described it as, 'perhaps the best, most comprehensive of any of the programs in my fifteen active years' Again you were the top rated speaker – two times at two EMI meetings in a three month period is something special. Your customized close of the challenges specific to our industry added that special touch.
    – J. H. Ebbinghaus, Vice President

Motorola, Inc.
Our recent sales events for the European Partner's and then the North American sales teams were the most positive ever. Your participation was a major contributor to these focused sessions. The feedback received was heartfelt and enthusiastic. The European session was well paced and understood given the fact that nine languages were represented in the group. We look forward to the opportunity to work with your organization in the future.
    – S. T. Morris, Director/Sales Programs, Computer
       Group

National Wooden Pallet and Container Association
I wish to thank you for your superb participation as the Keynoter for our annual meeting. You effectively captivated the attention of the audience. Their response was reflected in

the evaluations from the majority of those present who ranked your presentation as SUPERIOR. Your charismatic disposition made attending the meeting very enjoyable for our attendees. Many clamored for more... more... more! Thanks for making us look so good!

    – J. J. Healy, CAE, Executive Vice President

Sales and Marketing Executives of Fargo

It was truly a pleasure and an unexpected bonus to have a speaker that delivered not only what he promised and so much more! Your standard of excellence has been unmatched all year. Your program was the best received and STILL the most talked about seminar we have presented to the membership.

    – D. Trombley, SME Executive Secretary

CellularOne – GTE

You definitely delivered more than you promised to the 350 attendees at the GTE Wireless-Mid South Area Business Seminar. We have had more success stories in the weeks since, and I am sure that there will be many more to come. Your suggestions on how to be a successful sales professional really made an impact on the attendees, and I have seen much more 'out-of-the-box' ways to close sales since the seminar.

    – J. W. Cover, Manager, Distribution

Smith, Bucklin & Associates, Inc.

I found you to be an incredible presenter with a very important message. Yours was one of those sessions where I got great notes. I had some insightful and useful thoughts and inspirations of my own thanks to the tickling of my mind that you caused. Immediately, I came back and wanted to share with everyone that I know and care about. The evaluation is included. Everyone agrees with me!

    – D. Winterberg, Convention Manager

The Variable Annuity Life Insurance Company
On a scale of 1 to 10, Bill's comments on how to deliver outstanding customer service rate a 10. Several months prior to his speech, Bill spent the time necessary to learn our business. Consequently, his comments were right on target. His advice was perceptive, practical and directly relevant to our marketplace. If you have ever enjoyed the remarks of Somers White, Chris Hagerty or Harvey McKay, you'll like Bill Blades.
  – C. D. Robinson, CFP, Regional Manager

Wholesale Distributors Association
Your enthusiastic delivery kept everyone glued to your presentation and I've never seen so many people taking notes before. Our attendees rated you 10 – the highest level for exceeding their expectations.
  S. N. Erspamer, Executive Director

Retail Packaging Manufacturer's Association
Your presentation last week was excellent. But I'm sure you already know that. To share each and every one of the critiques with you would be extremely redundant. Almost every item was marked excellent and all comments were that the presentation was too short. I'm feeling quite fortunate right about now that I have the opportunity to bask in your glory by being responsible for making the choice to have you on our program.
  – V. Miller, Executive Director

Niagara Mohawk Power Corporation
Thank you very much for your challenging remarks on the importance of bringing joy and value to customers and for stretching our minds to think beyond the basic commodities in providing excellent electric and gas service.
  – W. L. Davis, Chairman of the Board and Chief
     Executive Officer

E-Z-GO Division of Textron, Inc.
What a great program you provided. Your talk was by far the 'highlight' of the three day meeting. Your common sense tips and tactics to improve everyone's selling skills was right on target and well received by our sales force.
— D. L. Davis, Director of Marketing

Dallas Wholesale Builders Supply, Inc.
Our company had a 26% jump in sales in 1994. This year, to date, we are running 35% ahead of 1994. I strongly feel Bill and the work he did for our organization helped light this 'fire'!
— B. Potter, President & Chief Executive Officer

National Sash and Door Jobbers Association
I just wanted to take this moment to drop you a note to thank you for your outstanding presentation. Your style and the content of your subject matter were excellent. I was particularly impressed with the manner in which you related to your audience during the presentation.
— R. T. O'Keefe, Chief Executive Officer, Executive Vice President

America West Airlines
Your stimulating speech, and the enthusiasm you generated by your approach to the sales mission, I applaud. I have seen many of our members already taking steps to put some of your ideas into action
— D. W. Ferguson, Director, Field Sales

National Poultry & Food Distributors Association
Thank you for a great seminar presentation. I heard a lot of positive comments about your presentation and even heard a few company CEO's discussing hiring you to visit and consult with their companies.
— K. McWhorter Braun, Executive Director

Floor Installation Association of North America

I want to thank you for a dynamic presentation. Your grasp of this subject is certainly better than any we've heard and you gave all our members, both Manufacturers and Distributors a lot to think about. You rated extremely high on our attendee's opinion forms.

– J. Lee, President

**To Book Bill Blades
and/or
To Purchase Products by Bill Blades
Found on Opposite Page**

Please contact:

William Blades
Phone: 480-563-5355
Fax: 480-563-0515
email: bill@williamblades.com
www.williamblades.com

EDUCATIONAL PRODUCTS

Audio Products
  Bill Blades Live (2 ½ hours)
  Effective Sales Management (8 hours)
  Professional Selling (4 hours)
  Proactive Leadership (4 hours)
  Growing Your Business (4 hours)
  Launching New Products (3 hours)

Video Products
  World-Class Service (30 minutes)
  Relationship Selling (30 minutes)
  Re-Energizing the Organization (4 tapes, 30 minutes)
  Crazee Selling (60 minutes)

Books
  Leadership Strategists (anthology)
  Top Gun Selling: Tactics of the Top 2% of Salespeople
      Replaces: Selling: The Mother of All Enterprise
  Break-out Creativity (anthology)
  Marketing for People Not in Marketing (anthology)
  Celebrate Selling (anthology)

Miscellaneous
  Motivation Coffee Cup

POWER PACKAGE!
Contains: All of the above audio products (6), Re-
             Energizing the Organization videos (4),
             Crazee Selling video and all 5 books.

             Call for latest price and we pay the freight!

  • Includes any shipping and handling in the United
    States only.